EVERYMAN, I will go with thee, and be thy guide,
In thy most need to go by thy side

DYLAN MARLAIS THOMAS was born in Swansea on 27
October 1914. After leaving school he worked briefly as
a junior reporter on the *South Wales Evening Post*
before embarking on a literary career in London. Here
he rapidly established himself as one of the finest poets
of his generation. *Eighteen Poems* appeared in 1934,
Twenty-five Poems in 1936, and *Deaths and Entrances*
in 1946; his *Collected Poems* were published in 1952.
Throughout his life Thomas wrote short stories, his
most famous collection being *Portrait of the Artist as a
Young Dog*. He also wrote filmscripts, broadcast stories
and talks, lectured in America, and wrote the radio play
Under Milk Wood. On 9 November 1953, shortly after
his thirty-ninth birthday, he collapsed and died in New
York. His body is buried in Laugharne, Wales, his home
for many years.

The Colour of Saying

Made in Great Britain by
Guernsey Press Co. Ltd, Guernsey, C.I. for
J. M. Dent & Sons Ltd
91 Clapham High Street, London SW4 7TA
First published by J.M. Dent 1963
Reprinted 1965, 1968, 1973, 1977, 1984
First published as an Everyman Classic 1989

No 1068 Paperback ISBN 0 460 01068 9

CONTENTS

[v]

[vi]

[vii]

[viii]

'*Once it was the colour of saying*
Soaked my table the uglier side of a hill
With a capsized field where a school sat still . . . .'

NOTE

THE editors have made every effort to make this anthology as complete and as comprehensive as possible, but problems of copyright have, in a very few cases, led to the exclusion of some pieces.

The editors wish to thank Miss Marion Jenkins and Miss Ceinwen Jones for their willing assistance in preparing the manuscript for the press.

Introduction

'LET'S EDIT a paper,' decide the two young men (aged fourteen) in the story 'The Fight' which is included in Dylan Thomas's intermittently autobiographical *Portrait of the Artist as a Young Dog*. While '*The Thunderer*, edited by D. Jenkyn Thomas', was rumbling in the Uplands, Swansea, there was on Mount Pleasant a real, if more pedestrian, magazine to be edited. Thomas became a sub-editor of the *Swansea Grammar School Magazine* with the issue of July 1929. As full editor in his final year at school (1930–1) he simplified the editorial function by writing practically the whole magazine himself. But the schoolboy audience was cramping, and on 2nd June 1931 the following paragraph appeared in the *South Wales Daily Post*:

A SWANSEA PUBLICATION

Some time ago it was announced in this column that Swansea might shortly expect a new literary publication, entitled *Prose and Verse*.

It is, as was then mentioned, to be published by subscription, and although the editor hopes to be able to reduce the price of subsequent issues, the price of the first copy is to be two shillings. It is necessary to sell at least two hundred copies at this price in order to cover the initial expenses.

The editor, who is to be found at 5 Cwmdonkin Drive, Uplands, wants contributions, and he says that 'their only qualification must be originality of outlook and expression'.

[xiii]

At least two Swansea people are known to have responded. One, Mr Emlyn Davies, a now retired music teacher in a local school, has the distinction—among other things—of having lived in 5 Cwmdonkin Drive since 1938 when Thomas's parents vacated it. The other, Mr Trevor Hughes, moved to London soon after the announcement, but kept in touch with Thomas by letter. Two years later Thomas was still thinking about the magazine:

> *Prose and Verse*, that stillborn child, is to be resurrected. Grocer Trick [A. E. 'Bert' Trick, well known in Swansea Labour Party circles] is to do the financial and business part of it, and I, as it was arranged before, am to edit it. The high standards formerly set will be strictly adhered to, but there is one important new condition. 'P & V' will print only the work of Welshmen and women and this includes those of dim Welsh ancestry and those born in Wales— who *write* in English. This condition necessarily restricts, but it is that which will make, I hope and trust, the journal an unique affair. Another highbrow periodical, especially produced from a blowsy town such as this—on the furthest peaks of the literary world—is damned to hell from the beginning. But a new high-class periodical for Welshmen? Up Cymru! I don't see why it shouldn't be a great success.

This was in October 1933; three months later the magazine was 'a sad story . . . no more than a legend for old men to tell their children'. But two months after that, early in March 1934, a letter to a new correspondent, the poet Glyn Jones, broached the same idea: 'At the moment I am attempting to form an anthology of English poems and stories written by contemporary Welshmen.' Another Welshman, Keidrych Rhys, had been thinking along the same lines, and in the Summer of 1937 produced the first issue of his very lively *Wales*. A Thomas story was featured on the front cover; and apparently Thomas had recruited other contributions—from Vernon Watkins, for instance. Writing to Watkins after the first issue, he envisaged closer ties with the magazine: 'Yes, I thought *Wales* was good, too. I had actually very little myself to do with the editing, though when Keidrych goes up to Cambridge next year I shall probably—and with you as colleague, or whatever it is, if you'd be—take it all over' (*Letters to Vernon Watkins*, p. 27). Thomas did go so far as to be listed as a co-editor in *Wales*, March 1939.

This active background with the writings of his contemporaries stood Thomas in good stead when he was finally encouraged to put together an anthology. The occasion was the 'London programme' referred to on p. 70 of the *Letters to Vernon Watkins*—readings of poems in the interval of a production of a Vernon Watkins masque, planned for the Mercury Theatre in London. On 23rd August 1939 Thomas sent to Mr Thomas Taig, the producer, a batch of poems 'that might be suitable for some kind of dramatic presentation', including the work of Glyn Jones, John Prichard, Keidrych Rhys, Ken Etheridge, Davies Aberpennar, Meurig Walters, George Woodcock, Alan Pryce Jones [1] and himself. In the covering letter Thomas offered his services as reader: 'I do hope you'll be able to give me the opportunity of reading: I enjoy reading poems aloud so much, and have got to understand most of the poems turned out nowadays by Our Young Welsh Poets'. The war called a halt to the production; so the *entr'acte* anthology remains an historical rather than a literary document, very much linked to its time and place ('I've included a few more-or-less-journalistic poems about distressed Wales').

[1] All these Welsh poets appear in Keidrych Rhys's anthology, *Modern Welsh Poetry*, Faber & Faber, 1944.

[xv]

The war also cancelled a broadcast Thomas was to have done with Keidrych Rhys to be called 'Modern Welsh Poets' scheduled for 6th September 1939. From October 1945 to October 1948, however, Thomas did over a hundred broadcasts, the great majority of them readings for producer John Arlott in a 'Book of Verse' series for the Overseas Service. These poetry programmes on one writer or one subject were edited by a variety of people. On 5th January 1946 Thomas edited one entitled 'Welsh Poets'. The talk, which he preferred to call 'an anthology with comments', can be found in the volume of broadcasts, *Quite Early One Morning*. Other such compilations by Thomas were Wilfred Owen, Sir Philip Sidney and Edward Thomas. Having no desire to remain typed as B.B.C. expert on the Anglo-Welsh, Thomas made several requests to read American writers. In July 1952 he recorded his choice from the poems of Robert Lowell and Theodore Roethke, and that summer produced a script, an introduction to and selections from Edgar Lee Masters's *Spoon River Anthology*, broadcast posthumously on 23rd January 1955. In a letter dated 15th July 1953 to Mr P. H. Newby of the B.B.C. Third Programme, Thomas was still hankering to do a more comprehensive reading of American poets.

.   .   .   .   .

The poems which comprise the present volume were chosen by Thomas in circumstances different from any mentioned above. They are taken from a number of sources; but in each case Thomas was clearly (*a*) making a free choice from the whole range of poetry in the English language, and (*b*) choosing poems that he especially liked (for one reason or another) and that he expected a general audience to enjoy in public readings.

The first major source is the series of four programmes called

'Anthologies', instigated by Aneirin Talfan Davies at the B.B.C. in Swansea and recorded there by Thomas on 9th and 10th February 1953, and transmitted on the four consecutive Sundays beginning 1st March 1953, St David's Day. The first anthology, deliberately Welsh, gives us the mature Thomas's final selection from the modern Welsh poets: W. H. Davies, Wilfred Owen, Edward Thomas, Alun Lewis, Idris Davies and Vernon Watkins. Also included here are poems recorded though not finally broadcast, and poems whose titles were jotted down by Thomas in preparation for the broadcasts.

The second major source is the stack of poems in manuscript left with the trustees of the Dylan Thomas Estate at the poet's death. Theodore Roethke, in Tedlock's *The Legend and the Poet* (p. 51), describes these documents:

> I noticed one day a big pile of poems—Edward Thomas, Hardy, Ransom, Housman, W. R. Rodgers, Davies and others—all copied out in his careful hand. He said he never felt he knew a poem, what was in it, until he had done this.

These transcriptions by hand, then, were Thomas's personal anthology. About eighty poems exist in this form, and naturally many of the poems he recited before British and American audiences can be found included.

Typical of Thomas's poetry readings (though exceptional in that tape recordings are preserved) were the two given at the Massachusetts Institute of Technology, Cambridge, Massachusetts. The first was on 7th March 1952 and was introduced by the remarks later printed in the *London Magazine* (September 1956) under the title 'I am going to read aloud'. The poets included were William Plomer, Henry Reed, Yeats, MacNeice, Auden and himself. For the second programme on 11th May 1953,

Thomas dropped his own poems completely and did a much more informal anthology, mainly of light verse not too well known. His introduction on this occasion was later revised for the B.B.C. and appears in *Quite Early One Morning* as 'A Visit to America'. Reference has also been made to the readings taped at the New York Y.M.H.A. Poetry Center (the selection broadcast by the B.B.C. Third Programme on 12th August 1956) and to the list of poems for reading contained in a manuscript now at the University of Buffalo, New York.

It was through the act of public reading, whether by radio or before a visible audience, that Thomas attained the phenomenal success which he achieved during his short lifetime, and which made tens of thousands of people, all over the world, feel his early death as a real personal loss.

The magic of that voice insinuated an ease of understanding into the most difficult of his poems, and his readings of other poets' work brought back a sense of enjoyment to the business of poetry which had been absent for some time. For Thomas *enjoyed* poetry, and his skill as a reader, allied to a voice of unusual richness, succeeded in communicating this enjoyment to the listener. His advice to a young inquirer was:

> Read the poems you like reading. Don't bother whether they're 'important', or if they'll live. What does it matter what poetry *is*, after all? If you want a definition of poetry, say: 'Poetry is what makes me laugh or cry or yawn, what makes my toenails twinkle, what makes me want to do this or that or nothing', and let it go at that.* [1]

This anthology is, we hope, a mirror of this belief.

[1] Quotations marked * are taken from the text printed in *Texas Quarterly*, vol. iv, No. 4.

That Thomas was a Welshman is not unimportant. To understand his particularly uninhibited approach to the reading of poetry it must be remembered that he was brought up in a community where the poet was still something of a public hero, and the publishing of a new poem something of an event. The art of public utterance was still at a premium in the Wales of his boyhood days. In the Welsh pulpit, oratory based on the majestic rhythms of the Welsh Bible and the mighty hymns of William Williams of Pantycelyn—Wales's greatest poet—were until recently the permanent background of a Welsh child's upbringing; and the oratory of the pulpit overspilled into the realm of politics, making of men like Lloyd George and Aneurin Bevan beings akin to gods in the eyes of the Welsh and objects of suspicion to the English over the border. As Thomas himself has said: 'The great rhythms [of the Bible] rolled over me from the Welsh pulpits. . . .' He was also fortunate in a father who was a passionate lover of poetry, and instilled this love into his son at a very early age. In a recently published manuscript of notes made in answer to queries about poetry, Thomas describes his first falling in love with nursery rhymes:

I had come to love just the words of them, the words alone. What the words stood for, symbolized or meant, was of very secondary importance; what mattered was the sound of them as I heard them for the first time on the lips of the remote and incomprehensible grown-ups who seemed, for some reason, to be living in my world.*

He talks of being at the mercy of words, 'though sometimes now, knowing a little of their behaviour very well, I think I can influence them slightly and have even learned to beat them now and then, which they appear to enjoy'.*

And it was knowing the behaviour of words which made him such a skilful interpreter of other poets' work. As has already been said, Thomas was in the habit of copying out, in his own hand, any poem he liked. Those poems he loved he knew with an insight born of a common bond of craftsmanship with their creators, and he bestowed upon them, in his reading, a loving care. No poem has been so lovingly interpreted as, for example, in his reading of Lawrence's 'Ship of death': that warm, rich, dark, soothing voice wrapping itself around every word and phrase, bringing them to life and making them stand and dance a slow moving pattern of sense and sound, which brings us as near as possible to the ecstasy of the creative act.

This was one of the most wonderful things about Thomas's reading of poetry—it conformed so closely, it seemed to the listener, to the very rhythm of creation. His sensitivity seemed to be such that it was possible for him to ally himself, as it were, with the poet in the very act of creating the poem; so that a reading of his became something more than an 'interpretation'; it became a revelation, a revealing of the mystery of this living thing—a poem.

It was this skill which, no doubt, led to the initial acceptance of his own more difficult poems, and in turn to his own realization of the need for an immediate impact of *meaning*. He himself offered the opinion that reading a poem aloud does bring one closer to the poet, and his work for radio certainly contributed something towards that greater simplification and clarity which are to be found in his later poems. We must not make too much of the point, but it is worth remembering; for he was not unaware of the dangers which beset the reader-aloud of poems. In introducing a reading of his own work he said:

[xx]

But, oh, the danger! For what a reader-aloud of his own poems so often does is to mawken or melodramatize them, making a single simple phrase break with the fears or throb with the terrors from which he deludes himself the phrase has been born. There is the other reader, of course, who manages, by studious flatness, semi-detachment, and an almost condescending undersaying of his poems, to give the impression that what he really means is: 'Great things, but my own' (*Quite Early One Morning*, p. 131).

But he did come to believe that there should be a great deal of 'meaning' available to the reader or listener at the first reading. During a lecture tour in America he was reported as saying:

It is impossible to be too clear. I am trying for more clarity now. At first I thought it enough to leave an impression of sound and feeling and let the meaning seep in later, but since I have been giving these broadcasts and reading other men's poetry as well as my own, I find it better to have more meaning at first reading (*Tedlock*, p. 62).

His technical skill in reading the most wide-ranging variety of poems was astounding. When recording the four anthologies for radio mentioned above, Thomas and the producer were standing in the studio, ready to record. The producer had a copy of Gerard Manley Hopkins's poems in his hand, and suddenly turned to the poet and asked him whether he would like to read 'The leaden echo and the golden echo'. It was not intended that he should read it there and then, but merely that he should make a mental note for future reference. But Thomas took hold of the book, drew his finger rapidly down the pages and in a second said: 'Yes, I'll do it now.' The red light flashed, and he proceeded to record this lovely poem, bringing it alive in all its intricate beauty. It was obvious that he had spent a great deal of time in the company of Hopkins.

It is true that he possessed a voice of amazing richness and power, and it is true also that he loved to use it in all its glorious resonance; but he never used it for empty mouthing. But when it was used with all the stops out, oh, how it thundered like a cathedral organ, filling all the 'holes and corners' of the universe of man. Anyone who has listened to his reading of Edith Sitwell's 'Still falls the rain' will remember the thrill of that sudden leap of the voice and ecstatic shout, as he came to Marlowe's lines which are used in the poem:

Then—O Ile leape up to my God: who pulles me doune—
See, see where Christ's blood streames in the firmament:

One of his finest recordings is the one of his own poem, 'Ceremony After a Fire Raid', with his voice rolling on to the tremendous liturgical climax in the magnificent last section of the poem, and the ecstasy of the thrice-pealed song of glory:

Glory, glory, glory
The sundering ultimate kingdom of genesis' thunder.

He found the reading of religious poems a congenial task, and it is doubtful whether W. R. Rodgers's moving poem to Mary Magdalene, 'Lent', has ever had a more sympathetic treatment than it got from Thomas's broadcast reading. Who better than he to interpret that mixture of sensuousness and humble adoration which this magnificent poem contains?

Over the balconies of these curved breasts
I'll no more peep to see
The light procession of my loves
Surf-riding in to me
Who now have eyes and alcoves, Lord, for Thee.

But it must be added that with a poem such as T. S. Eliot's 'Journey of the Magi' he was not altogether happy; although it must be said also that he thought much less of his reading of this poem than many of his listeners did. He seemed to feel that he had not the right voice for a poem which—so he said—needed an academic voice for reading it. His view may have been conditioned, however, by hearing Eliot's own reading of this poem.

We are not surprised to see W. B. Yeats well represented in his anthology, for his admiration of this poet was fairly well known, but the place given to Auden is a different matter. Thomas had always been held up as an example of the politically and socially uncommitted poet. He belonged to no political party. When he attended one of those so-called peace conferences in Prague, he shrugged the whole business off with a phrase: 'I was the only non-communist there!' If he could be labelled at all, which we doubt, 'anarchist' would be the nearest bet; but there is one safer bet, and that is that Thomas himself would throw it off with a shrug of those eloquent shoulders. He was committed to one thing only, and that was his 'craft and sullen art'. Any contribution which he had to make to the wellbeing of his fellow man had to come through his poetry. For he believed that poetry was important and that the poet had something to offer mankind—love. There was a terrifying fierceness in his voice when he read Auden's lines:

> This romantic lie in the brain
> Of the sensual man-in-the-street
> And the lie of Authority
> Whose buildings grope the sky:
> There is no such thing as the State
> And no one exists alone;

> Hunger allows no choice
> To the citizen or the police;
> We must love one another or die.

Thomas himself had attacked the romantic lie:

> Our eunuch dreams, all seedless in the light,
> Of light and love . . .
> In this our age the gunman and his moll,
> Two one-dimensional ghosts, love on a reel,
> Strange to our solid eye,
> And speak their midnight nothings as they swell . . .
> We watch the show of shadows kiss or kill,
> Flavoured of celluloid give love the lie. . . .

And his only answer to this negation of love is to affirm that:

> This is the world. Have faith.

It was a vision of the triumph of love which gave to his later and last poems their note of exaltation and blessedness:

> And this blessing most,
> That the closer I move
> To death, one man through his sundered hulks,
> The louder the sun blooms,
> And the tusked, ramshackling sea exults;
> And every wave of the way
> And gale I tackle, the whole world then,
> With more triumphant faith
> Than ever was since the world was said,
> Spins its morning of praise . . .

As we have already said, Thomas believed in poetry. 'Poetry, to a poet,' he has said, 'is the most rewarding work in the world. A good poem is a contribution to reality. The world is never the same once a good poem has been added to it. A good poem helps to change the shape and significance of the universe, helps to extend everyone's knowledge of himself and the world around him. . . .'*

Testimony to Dylan Thomas's success as a reader of other men's poems abounds. This anthology has been compiled in the belief that the choice of poems, as well as the reader's performance, ensured that success.

R. N. M.
A. T. D.

ACKNOWLEDGMENTS

FOR PERMISSION to reprint copyright material the cordial thanks of the editors and publishers are offered to the following:

Allen & Unwin Ltd and the author for 'Sacco writes to his son' and 'Song' from *Ha! Ha! Among the trumpets* by Alun Lewis; Edward Arnold Ltd for 'Opportunity' from *More Ruthless Rhymes* by Harry Graham; Jonathan Cape Ltd, Mrs H. M. Davies and the authors for 'The inquest', 'The poet' and 'One poet visits another' by W. H. Davies, 'A right of way: 1865' and 'The flying bum: 1944' by William Plomer, 'Naming of parts' and 'Chard Whitlow' by Henry Reed; Chatto & Windus, and the authors for 'It seemed that out of battle I escaped' from *Poems* by Wilfred Owen and 'The groundhog' from *Collected Poems* by Richard Eberhart; The Cresset Press for 'The watch' by Frances Cornford from her *Collected Poems*; the John Day Company for 'Song' from *Selected Verse* by John Manifold, copyright 1946 by the John Day Company; the author, J. M. Dent & Sons Ltd and Little, Brown & Co. Inc. for 'Very like a whale' by Ogden Nash, copyright 1946 by Ogden Nash; and J. M. Dent & Sons Ltd for 'O what can you give me' from *Gwalia Deserta* by Idris Davies; Gerald Duckworth & Co. Ltd for 'The garden party', 'Lord Finchley', 'Henry King' and 'Godolphin Horne' from *Cautionary Verses* by Hilaire Belloc; Faber & Faber Ltd and the authors for 'As I walked out . . .', 'September 1, 1939', 'O for doors to be open', 'Roman wall blues', 'The unknown citizen' and 'Victor' by W. H. Auden from his *Collected Poems*, 'To my mother' and 'News of the World II' by George Barker from his *Collected Poems*, 'Mythology' by Lawrence Durrell from his *Collected Poems*, 'The Journey of the Magi' by T. S. Eliot from his *Collected Poems*, 'The dead in Europe' and 'As a plane tree by the water' by Robert Lowell from *Poems, 1938–1949* (Canadian rights Harcourt, Brace in *Lord Weary's Castle*), 'The libertine' from *Collected Poems* and 'Suicide' from *Plant and Phantom* by Louis MacNeice, 'His shield' by Marianne Moore from her *Collected Poems* (Canada copyright 1951, The Macmillan Co.), 'A lover's words' and 'The collier' from *Ballad of the Mari Lwyd* by Vernon Watkins; the author for 'Raftery's dialogue with the whiskey' by Padraic Fallon; T. E. Hanley for the sentences from the *Texas Quarterly* quoted by the editors in their introduction; Rupert Hart-Davis Ltd for 'The buried child' by Lady Dorothy Wellesley, and 'Passing the graveyard', 'A prospect of death' and 'The shepherd's hut' by Andrew Young; William Heinemann Ltd and the author for 'The little brother' from *Collected Poems* by James Reeves; The Hutchinson Publishing Group and the author for 'O Boys! O Boys!' by Oliver St John Gogarty; the author for 'Esyllt' by Glyn Jones; the author for 'A Christmas childhood' by Patrick Kavanagh; Laurence Pollinger Ltd and the estate of the late Mrs Frieda Lawrence for 'End of another home holiday' and 'Ship of death' from the *Complete Poems of D. H. Lawrence*; Eyre & Spottiswoode Ltd and the author for 'Judith of Bethulia', 'Parting without a sequel' and 'Bells for John Whiteside's daughter' by John Crowe Ransom (reprinted from *Selected Poems* by John Crowe Ransom, by permission of Alfred A. Knopf Inc. Copyright 1924, 1927 by Alfred A. Knopf Inc. Renewed 1952, 1955 by

estate of the late A. E. Housman, and Messrs Jonathan Cape Ltd, publishers of A. E. Housman's *Collected Poems*, for 'Infant innocence'; Mrs Helen Thomas for 'The owl' and 'The unknown bird' by Edward Thomas; International Authors, N.Y. for 'Lollocks', 'The great-grandmother', 'The oldest soldier', 'Song: lift boy', 'Grotesques', 'Counting the beats', 'The bards' and 'The traveller's curse after misdirection' from Robert Graves' *Collected Poems* published by Cassell & Co; Miss D. E. Collins and Methuen & Co. Ltd for 'Wine and water' from *The Flying Inn* by G. K. Chesterton; Mrs W. B. Yeats and Macmillan & Co. Ltd for 'The three bushes', 'A dialogue of self and soul', 'Lapis lazuli', 'Three things', 'Endure what life God gives', 'John Kinsella's lament', 'For Anne Gregory' and 'He thinks of his past greatness' by W. B. Yeats; John Short for 'Carol'.

OBITUARY

*Max
Adeler*

Little Alexander's dead;
  Jam him in a coffin;
Don't have as good a chance
  For a fun'ral often.

Rush his body right around
  To the cemetery;
Drop him in the sepulchre
  With his Uncle Jerry.

IN MEMORIAM

*Max
Adeler*

Willie had a purple monkey climbing on a yellow
  stick,
And when he sucked the paint all off it made him
  deathly sick;
And in his latest hours he clasped that monkey in his
  hand,
And bid good-bye to earth and went into a better
  land.

Oh! no more he'll shoot his sister with his little
  wooden gun;
And no more he'll twist the pussy's tail and make her
  yowl, for fun.

[1]

The pussy's tail now stands out straight; the gun is
    laid aside;
The monkey doesn't jump around since little Willie
    died.

Anon.   POLLY PERKINS

I am a broken-hearted milkman, in grief I'm arrayed,
Through keeping of the company of a young servant
    maid,
Who lived on board wages to keep the house clean
In a gentleman's family near Paddington Green.

            She was as beautiful as a butterfly
                And as proud as a Queen
            Was pretty Polly Perkins of
                Paddington Green.

Her eyes were as black as the pips of a pear,
No rose in the garden with her cheeks could compare,
Her hair hung in ringlets so beautiful and long,
I thought that she loved me but I found I was wrong.

When I asked her to marry me she said, Oh! what
    stuff,
And told me to drop it, for she had quite enough
Of my nonsense—at the same time I'd been very
    kind,
But to marry a milkman she did not feel inclined.

[2]

Oh, the man that has me must have silver and gold,
A chariot to ride in and be handsome and bold,
His hair must be curly as any watch spring,
And his whiskers as long as a brush for clothing.

In six months she married, this hard-hearted girl,
But it was not a wicount, and it was not a nearl,
It was not a baronite, but a shade or two wuss,
It was a bow-legged conductor of a twopenny bus.

UNFORTUNATE MISS BAILEY   *Anon.*

A Captain bold from Halifax who dwelt in country
    quarters,
Betrayed a maid who hanged herself one morning in
    her Garters,
His wicked conscience smited him, he lost his stomach
    daily,
And took to drinking Ratafia while thinking of Miss
    Bailey.

One night betimes he went to bed, for he had caught
    a Fever;
Says he, 'I am a handsome man, but I'm a gay
    Deceiver.'
His candle just at twelve o'clock began to burn quite
    palely,
A Ghost stepped up to his bedside and said 'Behold
    Miss Bailey!'

'Avaunt, Miss Bailey!' then he cries, 'your Face
    looks white and mealy.'
'Dear Captain Smith,' the ghost replied, 'you've
    used me ungenteelly;
The Crowner's 'Quest goes hard with me because
    I've acted frailly,
And Parson Biggs won't bury me though I am dead
    Miss Bailey.'

'Dear Corpse!' said he, 'since you and I accounts
    must once for all close,
There really is a one pound note in my regimental
    small-clothes;
I'll bribe the sexton for your grave.' The ghost then
    vanished gaily
Crying 'Bless you, Wicked Captain Smith, remem-
    ber poor Miss Bailey.'

Anon.   THE HEARSE SONG

The old Grey Hearse goes rolling by,
You don't know whether to laugh or cry;
For you know some day it'll get you too,
And the hearse's next load may consist of you.

They'll take you out, and they'll lower you down,
While men with shovels stand all around;
They'll throw in dirt, and they'll throw in rocks,
And they won't give a damn if they break the box.

[4]

And your eyes drop out and your teeth fall in,
And the worms crawl over your mouth and chin;
They invite their friends and their friends' friends too,
And you look like hell when they're through with
  you.

TARPAULING JACKET

Anon.

I am a young jolly brisk sailor,
  Delights in all manner of sport,
When I'm in liquor I'm mellow,
  The girls I then merrily court.
But love is surrounded with trouble,
  And puts such strange thoughts in my head,
Is it not a terrible story,
  That love it should strike me stone dead?

Here's a health to my friends and acquaintance,
  When death for me it doth come,
And let them behave in their station
  And send me a cask of good rum,
Let it be good royal stingo,
  With three barrels of beer,
To make my friends the more welcome
  When they meet me at derry down fair.

Let there be six sailors to carry me,
  Let them be damnable drunk,
And as they are going to bury me,
  Let them fall down with my trunk.

[5]

Let there be no sighing and sobbing,
    But one single favour I crave,
Take me up in a tarpauling jacket,
    And fiddle and dance to my grave.

Anon.   FOGGY, FOGGY DEW

When I was a bachelor, I lived by myself
And I worked at the weaver's trade;
The only, only thing that I ever did wrong
Was to woo a fair young maid.
I wooed her in the winter time,
And in the summer too;
And the only, only thing that I ever did wrong
Was to keep her from the foggy, foggy dew.

One night she came to my bedside
Where I lay fast asleep;
She laid her head upon my bed,
And then began to weep.
She sighed, she cried, she damn near died,
She said—'What shall I do?'—
So I hauled her into bed and I covered up her head,
Just to save her from the foggy, foggy dew.

Oh, I am a bachelor, I live with my son,
And we work at the weaver's trade;
And every, every time that I look into his eyes,
He reminds me of that maid.

He reminds me of the winter time,
And of the summer too;
And the many, many times that I held her in my arms,
Just to keep her from the foggy, foggy dew.

GYPSIES IN THE WOOD

Anon.

My mother said that I never should
Play with the gypsies in the wood,
The wood was dark; the grass was green;
In came Sally with a tambourine,
I went to the sea—no ship to get across;
I paid ten shillings for a blind white horse;
I up on his back and was off in a crack,
Sally, tell my Mother I shall never come back.

AS I ROVED OUT

Anon.

As I roved out on a May morning,
Being in the youthful spring,
I leaned my back close to the garden wall
To hear the small birds sing;

And to hear two lovers talk, my dear,
To know what they would say,
That I might know a little of her mind
Before I would go away.

[7]

'Come sit you down, my heart,' he says,
'All on this pleasant green,
It's full three-quarters of a year and more
Since together you and I have been.'

'I will not sit on the grass,' she said,
'Now nor any other time,
For I hear you're engaged with another maid,
And your heart is no more of mine.

'Oh, I'll not believe what an old man says,
For his days are well nigh done,
Nor will I believe what a young man says,
For he's fair to many a one.

'But I will climb a high, high tree,
And rob a wild bird's nest,
And I'll bring back whatever I do find
To the arms I love the best,' she said,
'To the arms I love the best.'

Anon.   THE LILY AND THE ROSE

The maidens came
    When I was in my mother's bower,
I had all that I would.
    The bailey beareth the bell away;
    The lily, the rose, the rose I lay.

[8]

The silver is white, red is the gold;
The robes they lay in fold.
   The bailey beareth the bell away;
   The lily, the rose, the rose I lay.
And through the glass windows shines the sun.
How should I love, and I so young?
   The bailey beareth the bell away;
The lily, the rose, the rose I lay.

THE UNQUIET GRAVE   *Anon.*

'The wind doth blow today, my love,
   And a few small drops of rain;
I never had but one true-love,
   In cold grave she was lain.

'I'll do as much for my true-love
   As any young man may;
I'll sit and mourn all at her grave
   For a twelvemonth and a day.'

The twelvemonth and a day being up,
   The dead began to speak:
'Oh who sits weeping on my grave,
   And will not let me sleep?'

''Tis I, my love, sits on your grave,
   And will not let you sleep;
For I crave one kiss of your clay-cold lips,
   That is all I seek.'

'You crave one kiss of my clay-cold lips;
    But my breath smells earthy strong;
If you have one kiss of my clay-cold lips,
    Your time will not be long.

''Tis down in yonder garden green,
    Love, where we used to walk,
The finest flower that ere was seen
    Is withered to a stalk.

'The stalk is withered dry, my love,
    So will our hearts decay;
So make yourself content, my love,
    Till God calls you away.'

W. H.
Auden

SEPTEMBER 1, 1939

I sit in one of the dives
On Fifty-second Street
Uncertain and afraid
As the clever hopes expire
Of a low dishonest decade:
Waves of anger and fear
Circulate over the bright
And darkened lands of the earth,
Obsessing our private lives;
The unmentionable odour of death
Offends the September night.

Accurate scholarship can
Unearth the whole offence

[10]

From Luther until now
That has driven a culture mad,
Find what occurred at Linz,
What huge imago made
A psychopathic god:
I and the public know
What all schoolchildren learn,
Those to whom evil is done
Do evil in return.

Exiled Thucydides knew
All that a speech can say
About Democracy,
And what dictators do,
The elderly rubbish they talk
To an apathetic grave;
Analysed all in his book,
The enlightenment driven away,
The habit-forming pain,
Mismanagement and grief:
We must suffer them all again.

Into this neutral air
Where blind skyscrapers use
Their full height to proclaim
The strength of Collective Man,
Each language pours its vain
Competitive excuse:
But who can live for long
In an euphoric dream;
Out of the mirror they stare,

Imperialism's face
And the international wrong.

Faces along the bar
Cling to their average day:
The lights must never go out,
The music must always play,
All the conventions conspire
To make this fort assume
The furniture of home;
Lest we should see where we are,
Lost in a haunted wood,
Children afraid of the night
Who have never been happy or good.

The windiest militant trash
Important Persons shout
Is not so crude as our wish:
What mad Nijinsky wrote
About Diaghilev
Is true of the normal heart;
For the error bred in the bone
Of each woman and each man
Craves what it cannot have,
Not universal love
But to be loved alone.

From the conservative dark
Into the ethical life
The dense commuters come,
Repeating their morning vow:

'I *will* be true to the wife,
I'll concentrate more on my work,'
And helpless governors wake
To resume their compulsory game:
Who can release them now,
Who can reach the deaf,
Who can speak for the dumb?

All I have is a voice
To undo the folded lie,
The romantic lie in the brain
Of the sensual man-in-the-street
And the lie of Authority
Whose buildings grope the sky:
There is no such thing as the State
And no one exists alone;
Hunger allows no choice
To the citizen or the police;
We must love one another or die.

Defenceless under the night
Our world in stupour lies;
Yet, dotted everywhere,
Ironic points of light
Flash out wherever the Just
Exchange their messages:
May I, composed like them
Of Eros and of dust,
Beleaguered by the same
Negation and despair,
Show an affirming flame.

ROMAN WALL BLUES

W. H.
Auden

Over the heather the wet wind blows,
I've lice in my tunic and a cold in my nose.

The rain comes pattering out of the sky,
I'm a Wall soldier, I don't know why.

The mist creeps over the hard grey stone,
My girl's in Tungria; I sleep alone.

Aulus goes hanging around her place,
I don't like his manners, I don't like his face.

Piso's a Christian, he worships a fish;
There'd be no kissing if he had his wish.

She gave me a ring but I diced it away;
I want my girl and I want my pay.

When I'm a veteran with only one eye
I shall do nothing but look at the sky.

W. H.
Auden

SONG OF THE MASTER AND BOATSWAIN

At Dirty Dick's and Sloppy Joe's
    We drank our liquor straight,
Some went upstairs with Margery,
    And some, alas, with Kate;
And two by two like cat and mouse
The homeless played at keeping house.

There Wealthy Meg, the Sailor's Friend,
   And Marion, cow-eyed,
Opened their arms to me but I
   Refused to step inside;
I was not looking for a cage
In which to mope in my old age.

The nightingales are sobbing in
   The orchards of our mothers,
And hearts that we broke long ago
   Have long been breaking others;
Tears are round, the sea is deep:
Roll them overboard and sleep.

O FOR DOORS TO BE OPEN

*W. H.
Auden*

O for doors to be open and an invite with gilded edges
To dine with Lord Lobcock and Count Asthma on
   the platinum benches,
With the somersaults and fireworks, the roast and the
   smacking kisses—
     Cried the cripples to the silent statue,
     The six beggared cripples.

And Garbo's and Cleopatra's wits to go astraying,
In a feather ocean with me to go fishing and playing
Still jolly when the cock has burst himself with crow-
   ing—
     Cried the six cripples to the silent statue,
     The six beggared cripples.

And to stand on green turf among the craning yellow
    faces,
Dependant on the chestnut, the sable, and Arabian
    horses,
And me with a magic crystal to foresee their places—
       Cried the six cripples to the silent statue,
       The six beggared cripples.

And this square to be a deck, and these pigeons sails
    to rig
And to follow the delicious breeze like a tantony pig
To the shaded feverless islands where the melons are
    big—
       Cried the six cripples to the silent statue,
       The six beggared cripples.

And these shops to be turned to tulips in a garden
    bed,
And me with my stick to thrash each merchant dead
As he pokes from a flower his bald and wicked
    head—
       Cried the six cripples to the silent statue,
       The six beggared cripples.

And a hole in the bottom of heaven, and Peter and
    Paul
And each smug surprised saint like parachutes to fall,
And every one-legged beggar to have no legs at all—
       Cried the six cripples to the silent statue,
       The six beggared cripples.

ONE EVENING

As I walked out one evening,
  Walking down Bristol Street,
The crowds upon the pavement
  Were fields of harvest wheat.

W. H. Auden

And down by the brimming river
  I heard a lover sing
Under an arch of the railway:
  'Love has no ending.

'I'll love you, dear, I'll love you
  Till China and Africa meet,
And the river jumps over the mountain
  And the salmon sing in the street.

'I'll love you till the ocean
  Is folded and hung up to dry,
And the seven stars go squawking
  Like geese about the sky.

'The years shall run like rabbits,
  For in my arms I hold
The Flower of the Ages,
  And the first love of the world.'

But all the clocks in the city
  Began to whirr and chime:
'O let not Time deceive you,
  You cannot conquer Time.

'In the burrows of the Nightmare
  Where Justice naked is,
Time watches from the shadow
  And coughs when you would kiss.

'In headaches and in worry
  Vaguely life leaks away,
And Time will have his fancy
  Tomorrow or today.

'Into many a green valley
  Drifts the appalling snow;
Time breaks the threaded dances
  And the diver's brilliant bow.

'O plunge your hands in water,
  Plunge them in up to the wrist;
Stare, stare in the basin
  And wonder what you've missed.

'The glacier knocks in the cupboard,
  The desert sighs in the bed,
And the crack in the tea-cup opens
  A lane to the land of the dead.

'Where the beggars raffle the banknotes
  And the Giant is enchanting to Jack,
And the Lily-white Boy is a Roarer,
  And Jill goes down on her back.

[18]

'O look, look in the mirror,
   O look in your distress;
Life remains a blessing
   Although you cannot bless.

'O stand, stand at the window
   As the tears scald and start;
You shall love your crooked neighbour
   With your crooked heart.'

It was late, late in the evening
   The lovers they were gone;
The clocks had ceased their chiming,
   And the deep river ran on.

VICTOR. A BALLAD

W. H.
Auden

Victor was a little baby,
   Into this world he came;
His father took him on his knee and said:
   'Don't dishonour the family name.'

Victor looked up at his father
   Looked up with big round eyes:
His father said; 'Victor, my only son,
   Don't you ever ever tell lies.'

Victor and his father went riding
    Out in a little dog-cart;
His father took a Bible from his pocket and read:
    'Blessed are the pure in heart.'

It was a frosty December,
    It wasn't the season for fruits;
His father fell dead of heart's disease
    While lacing up his boots.

It was a frosty December
    When into his grave he sank;
His uncle found Victor a post as cashier
    In the Midland Counties Bank.

It was a frosty December
    Victor was only eighteen,
But his figures were neat and his margins straight
    And his cuffs were always clean.

He took a room at the Peveril,
    A respectable boarding-house;
And Time watched Victor day after day
    As a cat will watch a mouse.

The clerks slapped Victor on the shoulder;
    'Have you ever had a woman?' they said,
'Come down town with us on Saturday night.'
    Victor smiled and shook his head.

The manager sat in his office,
    Smoked a Corona cigar:
Said: 'Victor's a decent fellow but
    He's too mousey to go far.'

Victor went up to his bedroom,
    Set the alarum bell;
Climbed into bed, took his Bible and read
    Of what happened to Jezebel.

It was the First of April,
    Anna to the Peveril came;
Her eyes, her lips, her breasts, her hips
    And her smile set men aflame.

She looked as pure as a schoolgirl
    On her First Communion day,
But her kisses were like the best champagne
    When she gave herself away.

It was the Second of April,
    She was wearing a coat of fur;
Victor met her upon the stairs
    And he fell in love with her.

The first time he made his proposal,
    She laughed, said: 'I'll never wed';
The second time there was a pause;
    Then she smiled and shook her head.

Anna looked into her mirror,
    Pouted and gave a frown:
Said: 'Victor's as dull as a wet afternoon
    But I've got to settle down.'

The third time he made his proposal,
    As they walked by the Reservoir:
She gave him a kiss like a blow on the head,
    Said: 'You are my heart's desire.'

They were married early in August,
    She said: 'Kiss me, you funny boy.'
Victor took her in his arms and said:
    'O my Helen of Troy.'

It was the middle of September,
    Victor came to the office one day;
He was wearing a flower in his buttonhole,
    He was late but he was gay.

The clerks were talking of Anna,
    The door was just ajar:
One said: 'Poor old Victor, but where ignorance
    Is bliss, etcetera.'

Victor stood still as a statue,
    The door was just ajar:
One said: 'God, what fun I had with her
    In that Baby Austin car.'

Victor walked out into the High Street,
   He walked to the edge of the town;
He came to the allotments and the rubbish heaps
   And his tears came tumbling down.

Victor looked up at the sunset
   As he stood there all alone;
Cried: 'Are you in Heaven, Father?'
   But the sky said: 'Address not known.'

Victor looked up at the mountains,
   The mountains all covered with snow;
Cried: 'Are you pleased with me, Father?'
   And the answer came back, 'No.'

Victor came to the forest,
   Cried: 'Father, will she ever be true?'
And the oaks and the beeches shook their heads
   And they answered: 'Not to you.'

Victor came to the meadow
   Where the wind went sweeping by;
Cried: 'O Father, I love her so,'
   But the wind said: 'She must die.'

Victor came to the river
   Running so deep and so still;
Crying: 'O Father, what shall I do?'
   And the river answered, 'Kill.'

Anna was sitting at table,
   Drawing cards from a pack;
Anna was sitting at table
   Waiting for her husband to come back.

It wasn't the Jack of Diamonds
   Nor the Joker she drew at first;
It wasn't the King or the Queen of Hearts
   But the Ace of Spades reversed.

Victor stood in the doorway,
   He didn't utter a word;
She said: 'What's the matter, darling?'
   He behaved as if he hadn't heard.

There was a voice in his left ear,
   There was a voice in his right,
There was a voice at the base of his skull
   Saying: 'She must die tonight.'

Victor picked up a carving-knife,
   His features were set and drawn,
Said: 'Anna, it would have been better for you
   If you had not been born.'

Anna jumped up from the table,
   Anna started to scream,
But Victor came slowly after her
   Like a horror in a dream.

She dodged behind the sofa,
  She tore down a curtain rod,
But Victor came slowly after her;
  Said: 'Prepare to meet thy God.'

She managed to wrench the door open,
  She ran and she didn't stop.
But Victor followed her up the stairs
  And he caught her at the top.

He stood there above the body,
  He stood there holding the knife;
And the blood ran down the stairs and sang,
  'I'm the Resurrection and the Life.'

They tapped Victor on the shoulder,
  They took him away in a van;
He sat as quiet as a lump of moss
  Saying: 'I am the Son of Man.'

Victor sat in a corner
  Making a woman of clay;
Saying: 'I am Alpha and Omega, I shall come
  To judge the earth one day.'

THE UNKNOWN CITIZEN

(To JS/07/M/378)

This Marble Monument
Is Erected by the State

W. H.
Auden

He was found by the Bureau of Statistics to be
One against whom there was no official complaint,
And all the reports on his conduct agree
That, in the modern sense of an old-fashioned word,
    he was a saint,
For in everything he did he served the Greater
    Community.
Except for the War till the day he retired
He worked in a factory and never got fired,
But satisfied his employers, Fudge Motors Inc.
Yet he wasn't a scab or odd in his views,
For his Union reports that he paid his dues,
(Our report on his Union shows it was sound)
And our Social Psychology workers found
That he was popular with his mates and liked a drink.
The Press are convinced that he bought a paper every
    day
And that his reactions to advertisements were normal
    in every way.
Policies taken out in his name prove that he was fully
    insured,
And his Health-card shows he was once in hospital
    but left it cured.
Both Producers Research and High-Grade Living
    declare
He was fully sensible to the advantages of the Instal-
    ment Plan

[26]

And had everything necessary to the Modern Man,
A phonograph, a radio, a car and a frigidaire.
Our researchers into Public Opinion are content
That he held the proper opinions for the time of year;
When there was peace, he was for peace; when there
    was war, he went.
He was married and added five children to the
    population,
Which our Eugenist says was the right number for a
    parent of his generation,
And our teachers report that he never interfered with
    their education.
Was he free? Was he happy? The question is absurd:
Had anything been wrong, we should certainly have
    heard.

SOB, HEAVY WORLD

*W. H.
Auden*

    Sob, heavy world,
    Sob as you spin
Mantled in mist, remote from the happy:
The washerwomen have wailed all night,
The disconsolate clocks are crying together,
    And the bells toll and toll
For tall Agrippa who touched the sky:
    Shut in that shining eye
Which enlightened the lampless and lifted up
The flat and foundering, reformed the weeds
Into civil cereals and sobered the bulls;

Away the cylinder seal,
The didactic digit and dreaded voice
Which imposed peace on the pullulating
Primordial mess. Mourn for him now,
    Our lost dad,
    Our colossal father.

    For seven cycles
    For seven years
Past vice and virtue, surviving both,
Through pluvial periods, paroxysms
Of wind and wet, through whirlpools of heat,
    And comas of deadly cold,
On an old white horse, an ugly nag,
    In his faithful youth he followed
The black ball as it bowled downhill
On the spotted spirit's spiral journey,
Its purgative path to that point of rest
    Where longing leaves it, and saw
Shimmering in the shade the shrine of gold,
The magical marvel no man dare touch,
Between the towers the tree of life
    And the well of wishes
    The waters of joy.

    Then he harrowed hell,
    Healed the abyss
Of torpid instinct and trifling flux,
Laundered it, lighted it, made it lovable with
Cathedrals and theories; thanks to him
    Brisker smells abet us,

Cleaner clouds accost our vision
    And honest sounds our ears.
For he ignored the Nightmares and annexed
    their ranges,
Put the clawing Chimaeras in cold storage,
Berated the Riddle till it roared and fled,
    Won the Battle of Whispers,
Stopped the Stupids, stormed into
The Fumblers' Forts, confined the Sulky
To their drab ditches and drove the Crashing
    Bores to their bogs,
    Their beastly moor.

    In the high heavens,
    The ageless places,
The gods are wringing their great worn hands
For their watchman is away, their world-engine
Creaking and cracking. Conjured no more
    By his master music to wed
Their truths to times, the Eternal Objects
    Drift about in a daze:
O the lepers are loose in Lombard Street,
The rents are rising in the river basins,
The insects are angry. Who will dust
    The cobwebbed kingdoms now?
For our lawgiver lies below his people,
Bigger bones of a better kind,
Unwarped by their weight, as white limestone
    Under green grass,
    The grass that fades.

TO MY MOTHER

Most near, most dear, most loved and most far,
Under the window where I often found her
Sitting as huge as Asia, seismic with laughter,
Gin and chicken helpless in her Irish hand,
Irresistible as Rabelais, but most tender for
The lame dogs and hurt birds that surround her,—
She is a procession no one can follow after
But be like a little dog following a brass band.

She will not glance up at the bomber, or condescend
To drop her gin and scuttle to a cellar,
But lean on the mahogany table like a mountain
Whom only faith can move, and so I send
O all my faith and all my love to tell her
That she will move from mourning into morning.

George
Barker

NEWS OF THE WORLD II

George
Barker

In the first year of the last disgrace
    Peace, turning her face away,
Coughing in laurelled fires, weeping,
    Drags out from her hatcheted heart
    The sunset axe of the day.

And leaning up against the red sky
    She mourns over evening cities:
The milky morning springs from her mothering breast
    Half choked with happy memories
    And fulfilment of miseries.

'I am the wife of the workman world
  With an apron full of children—
And happy, happy any hovel was
  With my helping hand under his gifted head
  And for my sleep his shoulder.

'I wish that the crestfallen stars would fall
  Out of his drunken eye and strike
My children cold. I wish the big sea
  Would pity them, and pity me,
  And smother us all alike.

'Bitter sun, bitter sun, put out your lions
  As I have put out my hope.
For he will take them in his clever hand
And teach them how to dismember love
  Just as though it was Europe.

'O washing-board Time, my hands are sore
  And the backs of the angels ache.
For the redhanded husband has abandoned me
To drag his coat in front of his pride,
  And I know my heart will break.'

In the first year of the last disgrace
  Peace, turning her face away,
Coughing in fire and laurels, weeping,
  Bared again her butchered heart
  To the sunrise axe of the day.

LORD FINCHLEY

Lord FINCHLEY tried to mend the Electric Light
Himself. It struck him dead: And serve him right!
It is the business of the wealthy man
To give employment to the artisan.

Hilaire
Belloc

Hilaire
Belloc

HENRY KING

Who chewed bits of String, and was early
cut off in Dreadful Agonies

The Chief Defect of Henry King
Was chewing little bits of String.
At last he swallowed some which tied
Itself in ugly Knots inside.
Physicians of the Utmost Fame
Were called at once; but when they came
They answered, as they took their Fees,
'There is no cure for this Disease.
Henry will very soon be dead.'
His Parents stood about his Bed
Lamenting his Untimely Death,
When Henry, with his Latest Breath
Cried—'Oh, my friends, be warned by me,
That Breakfast, Dinner, Lunch, and Tea
Are all the Human Frame requires. . . .'
With that, the Wretched Child expires.

[32]

THE GARDEN PARTY

The Rich arrived in pairs
And also in Rolls Royces;
They talked of their affairs
In loud and strident voices.

*Hilaire
Belloc*

(The Husbands and the Wives
Of this select society
Lead independent lives
Of infinite variety.)

The Poor arrived in Fords,
Whose features they resembled;
They laughed to see so many Lords
And Ladies all assembled.

The People in Between
Looked underdone and harassed
And out of place and mean,
And horribly embarrassed.

For the hoary social curse
Gets hoarier and hoarier,
And it stinks a trifle worse
Than in the days of Queen Victoria,

When they married and gave in marriage,
They danced at the County Ball,
And some of them kept a carriage,
And the flood destroyed them all.

GODOLPHIN HORNE

Who was cursed with the sin of Pride,
and Became a Boot-Black

Hilaire
Belloc

Godolphin Horne was Nobly Born;
He held the Human Race in Scorn,
And lived with all his Sisters where
His father lived, in Berkeley Square,
And oh! the Lad was Deathly Proud!
He never shook your Hand or Bowed,
But merely smirked and nodded thus:
How perfectly ridiculous!
Alas! That such Affected Tricks
Should flourish in a Child of Six!
(For such was Young Godolphin's age.)
Just then, the Court required a Page,
Whereat the Lord High Chamberlain
(The Kindest and the Best of Men)
He went good-naturedly and took
A Perfectly Enormous Book
Called *People Qualified to Be*
Attendant on His Majesty,
And murmured, as he scanned the list
(To see that no one should be missed),
'There's William Coutts has got the Flu,
And Billy Higgs would never do,
And Guy de Vere is far too young,
And ... wasn't D'Alton's Father hung?
And as for Alexander Byng! ...
I think I know the kind of thing,

[34]

A Churchman, clearly, nobly born,
Come let us say Godolphin Horne?'
But hardly had he said the word
When Murmurs of Dissent were heard.
The King of Iceland's Eldest Son
Said, 'Thank you! I am taking none!'
The Aged Duchess of Athlone
Remarked, in her sub-acid tone,
'I doubt if He is what we need!'
With which the Bishops all agreed;
And even Lady Mary Flood
(*So* Kind and oh! so *really* good)
Said: 'No! He wouldn't do at all,
He'd make us feel a lot too small.'
The Chamberlain said: '. . . Well, well, well!
No doubt you're right . . . One cannot tell!'
He took his Gold and Diamond Pen
And Scratched Godolphin out again.
So now Godolphin is the Boy
Who blacks the Boots at the Savoy.

A CHILD ILL

*John
Betjeman*

Oh, little body, do not die.
  The soul looks out through wide blue eyes
So questioningly into mine,
  That my tormented soul replies:

'Oh, little body, do not die.
  You hold the soul that talks to me
Although our conversation be
  As wordless as the windy sky.'

So looked my father at the last
  Right in my soul, before he died,
Though words we spoke went heedless past
  As London traffic-roar outside.

And now the same blue eyes I see
  Look through me from a little son,
So questioning, so searchingly
  That youthfulness and age are one.

My father looked at me and died
  Before my soul made full reply.
Lord, leave this other Light alight—
  Oh, little body, do not die.

THE ARREST OF OSCAR WILDE
AT THE CADOGAN HOTEL

He sipped at a weak hock and seltzer
  As he gazed at the London skies
Through the Nottingham lace of the curtains
  Or was it his bees-winged eyes?

*John
Betjeman*

To the right and before him Pont Street
  Did tower in her new built red,
As hard as the morning gaslight
  That shone on his unmade bed,

'I want some more hock in my seltzer,
  And Robbie, please give me your hand—
Is this the end or beginning?
  How can I understand?

'So you've brought me the latest *Yellow Book*:
  And Buchan has got in it now:
Approval of what is approved of
  Is as false as a well-kept vow.

'More hock, Robbie—where is the seltzer?
  Dear boy, pull again at the bell!
They are all little better than *cretins*,
  Though this *is* the Cadogan Hotel.

[37]

'One astrakhan coat is at Willis's—
    Another one's at the Savoy:
Do fetch my morocco portmanteau,
    And bring them on later, dear boy.'

A thump, and a murmur of voices—
    ('Oh why must they make such a din?')
As the door of the bedroom swung open
    And TWO PLAIN CLOTHES POLICEMEN came in:

'Mr Woilde, we 'ave come for tew take yew
    Where felons and criminals dwell:
We must ask yew tew leave with us quoietly
    For this *is* the Cadogan Hotel.'

He rose, and he put down *The Yellow Book*.
    He staggered—and, terrible-eyed,
He brushed past the palms on the staircase
    And was helped to a hansom outside.

POT POURRI FROM A SURREY GARDEN

Miles of pram in the wind and Pam in the gorse track,
    Coconut smell of the broom, and a packet of
      Weights
Press'd in the sand. The thud of a hoof on a horse-
    track—
      A horse-riding horse for a horse-track—
      Conifer county of Surrey approached
    Through remarkable wrought-iron gates.

Over your boundary now, I wash my face in a bird-
    bath,
      Then which path shall I take? that over there by
      the pram?
Down by the pond! or—yes, I will take the slippery
    third path,
      Trodden away with gym shoes,
      Beautiful fir-dry alley that leads
    To the bountiful body of Pam.

Pam, I adore you, Pam, you great big mountainous
    sports girl,
      Whizzing them over the net, full of the strength
      of five:
That Old Malvernian brother, you zephyr and khaki
    shorts girl,
      Although he's playing for Woking,
      Can't stand up
    To your wonderful backhand drive.

*John
Betjeman*

[39]

See the strength of her arm, as firm and hairy as
      Hendren's;
            See the size of her thighs, the pout of her lips as,
                  cross,
And full of a pent-up strength, she swipes at the
      rhododendrons,
            Lucky the rhododendrons,
            And flings her arrogant love-lock
      Back with a petulant toss.

Over the redolent pinewoods, in at the bathroom
      casement,
            One fine Saturday, Windlesham bells shall call:
Up the Butterfield aisle rich with Gothic enlacement,
            Licensed now for embracement,
            Pam and I, as the organ
      Thunders over you all.

SENEX

*John
Betjeman*

Oh would I could subdue the flesh
      Which sadly troubles me!
And then perhaps could view the flesh
As though I never knew the flesh
      And merry misery.

To see the golden hiking girl
      With wind about her hair,
The tennis-playing, biking girl,
The wholly-to-my-liking girl,
      To see and not to care.

At sundown on my tricycle
  I tour the Borough's edge,
And icy as an icicle
See bicycle by bicycle
  Stacked waiting in the hedge.

Get down from me! I thunder there,
  You spaniels! Shut your jaws!
Your teeth are stuffed with underwear,
Suspenders torn asunder there
  And buttocks in your paws!

Oh whip the dogs away, my Lord,
  They make me ill with lust.
Bend bare knees down to pray, my Lord,
Teach sulky lips to say, my Lord,
  That flaxen hair is dust.

THE BURNING OF THE LEAVES

Laurence Binyon

Now is the time for the burning of the leaves.
They go to the fire; the nostril pricks with smoke
Wandering slowly into the weeping mist.
Brittle and blotched, ragged and rotten sheaves!
A flame seizes the smouldering ruin and bites
On stubborn stalks that crackle as they resist.

The last hollyhock's fallen tower is dust;
All the spices of June are a bitter reek,
All the extravagant riches spent and mean.

[41]

All burns! the reddest rose is a ghost;
Sparks whirl up, to expire in the mist: the wild
Fingers of fire are making corruption clean.

Now is the time for stripping the spirit bare,
Time for the burning of days ended and done,
Idle solace of things that have gone before:
Rootless hope and fruitless desire are there;
Let them go to the fire, with never a look behind.
That world that was ours is a world that is ours no
    more.

They will come again, the leaf and the flower, to arise
From squalor of rottenness into the old splendour,
And magical scents to a wondering memory bring;
The same glory, to shine upon different eyes.
Earth cares for her own ruins, naught for ours.
Nothing is certian, only the certain spring.

Samuel
Butler

O GOD! O MONTREAL!

Stowed away in a Montreal lumber room
The Discobolus standeth and turneth his face to the
    wall;
Dusty, cobweb-covered, maimed and set at naught,
Beauty lieth in an attic and no man regardeth:
            O God! O Montreal!

Beautiful by night and day, beautiful in summer and
    winter,
Whole or maimed, always and alike beautiful—

He preacheth gospel of grace to the skins of owls
And to one who seasoneth the skins of Canadian
owls;
O God! O Montreal!

When I saw him I was wroth and I said, 'O Disco-
bolus!
Beautiful Discobolus, a Prince both among Gods and
men,
What doest thou here, how camest thou hither,
Discobolus,
Preaching gospel in vain to the skins of owls?'
O God! O Montreal!

And I turned to the man of skins and said unto him,
'O thou man of skins,
Wherefore hast thou done thus to shame the beauty
of the Discobolus?'
But the Lord had hardened the heart of the man of
skins,
And he answered, 'My brother-in-law is haberdasher
to Mr Spurgeon.'
O God! O Montreal!

'The Discobolus is put here because he is vulgar,
He has neither vest nor pants with which to cover his
limbs;
I, Sir, am a person of most respectable connections—
My brother-in-law is haberdasher to Mr Spurgeon.'
O God! O Montreal!

[43]

Then I said, 'O brother-in-law to Mr Spurgeon's
   haberdasher,
Who seasonest also the skins of Canadian owls,
Thou callest trousers 'pants', whereas I call them
   'trousers',
Therefore, thou art in hell-fire and may the Lord pity
   thee!'
                    O God! O Montreal!

'Preferrest thou the gospel of Montreal to the gospel
   of Hellas,
The gospel of thy connection with Mr Spurgeon's
   haberdashery to the gospel of the Discobolus?'
Yet none the less blasphemed he beauty saying: 'The
   Discobolus hath no gospel,
But my brother-in-law is haberdasher to Mr Spur-
   geon.'
                    O God! O Montreal!

STANZAS FOR MUSIC

There be none of Beauty's daughters
 With a magic like thee;
And like music on the waters
 Is thy sweet voice to me:
When, as if its sound were causing
The charmèd Ocean's pausing,
The waves lie still and gleaming,
And the lulled winds seem dreaming:
And the Midnight Moon is weaving
 Her bright chain o'er the deep;
Whose breast is gently heaving,
 As an infant's asleep:
So the spirit bows before thee,
To listen and adore thee;
With a full but soft emotion,
Like the swell of Summer's ocean.

Lord Byron

THE GOOD RICH MAN

G. K.
Chesterton

Mr Mandragon, the Millionaire, he wouldn't have
    wine or wife,
He couldn't endure complexity; he lived the simple
    life.
He ordered his lunch by megaphone in manly, simple
    tones,
And used all his motors for canvassing voters, and
    twenty telephones;
Besides a dandy little machine,
Cunning and neat as ever was seen
With a hundred pulleys and cranks between,
Made of metal and kept quite clean,
To hoist him out of his healthful bed on every day
    of his life,
And wash him and brush him, and shave him and
    dress him to live the Simple Life.

Mr Mandragon was most refined and quietly, neatly
    dressed,
Say all the American newspapers that know refine-
    ment best;
Neat and quiet the hair and hat, and the coat quiet
    and neat.
A trouser worn upon either leg, while boots adorn
    the feet;
And not, as any one might expect,
A Tiger Skin, all striped and flecked,
And a Peacock Hat with the tail erect,
A scarlet tunic with sunflowers decked,

That might have had a more marked effect,
And pleased the pride of a weaker man that yearned
   for wine or wife;
But fame and the flagon, for Mr Mandragon obscured
   the Simple Life.

Mr Mandragon, the Millionaire, I am happy to say, is
   dead;
He enjoyed a quiet funeral in a crematorium shed,
And he lies there fluffy and soft and grey, and cer-
   tainly quite refined,
When he might have rotted to flowers and fruit with
   Adam and all mankind,
Or been eaten by wolves athirst for blood,
Or burnt on a big tall pyre of wood,
In a towering flame, as a heathen should,
Or even sat with us here at food,
Merrily taking twopenny ale and cheese with a
   pocket-knife;
But these were luxuries not for him who went for the
   Simple Life.

THE WATCH

*Frances
Cornford*

I wakened on my hot, hard bed,
Upon the pillow lay my head;
Beneath the pillow I could hear
My little watch was ticking clear.
I thought the throbbing of it went
Like my continual discontent;

[47]

I thought it said in every tick:
I am so sick, so sick, so sick;
O death, come quick, come quick, come quick,
Come quick, come quick, come quick, come quick.

VOYAGES II

Hart Crane

And yet this great wink of eternity,
Of rimless floods, unfettered leewardings,
Samite sheeted and processioned where
Her undinal vast belly moonward bends,
Laughing the wrapt inflections of our love;

Take this Sea, whose diapason knells
On scrolls of silver snowy sentences,
The sceptred terror of whose sessions rends
As her demeanours motion well or ill,
All but the pieties of lovers' hands.

And onward, as bells off San Salvador
Salute the crocus lustres of the stars,
In these poinsettia meadows of her tides,—
Adagios of islands, O my Prodigal,
Complete the dark confessions her veins spell.

Mark how her turning shoulders wind the hours,
And hasten while her penniless rich palms
Pass superscription of bent foam and wave,—
Hasten, while they are true,—sleep, death, desire,
Close round one instant in one floating flower.

Bind us in time, O Seasons clear, and awe.
O minstrel galleons of Carib fire,
Bequeath us to no earthly shore until
Is answered in the vortex of our grave
The seal's wide spindrift gaze toward paradise.

FROM 'GWALIA DESERTA'

*Idris
Davies*

O what can you give me?
Say the sad bells of Rhymney.

Is there hope for the future?
Cry the brown bells of Merthyr.

Who made the mineowner?
Say the black bells of Rhondda.

And who robbed the miner?
Cry the grim bells of Blaina.

They will plunder willy-nilly,
Say the bells of Caerphilly.

They have fangs, they have teeth!
Shout the loud bells of Neath.

To the south, things are sullen,
Say the pink bells of Brecon.

Even God is uneasy,
Say the moist bells of Swansea.

Put the vandals in court!
Cry the bells of Newport.

All would be well if-if-if-
Say the green bells of Cardiff.

Why so worried, sisters, why?
Sing the silver bells of Wye.

THE INQUEST

*W. H.
Davies*

I took my oath I would inquire,
    Without affection, hate, or wrath,
Into the death of Ada Wright—
    So help me God! I took that oath.

When I went out to see the corpse,
    The four months' babe that died so young,
I judged it was seven pounds in weight,
    And little more than one foot long.

One eye, that had a yellow lid,
    Was shut—so was the mouth, that smiled;
The left eye open, shining bright—
    It seemed a knowing little child.

For as I looked at that one eye,
    It seemed to laugh, and say with glee:
'What caused my death you'll never know—
    Perhaps my mother murdered me.'

When I went into court again,
        To hear the mother's evidence—
It was a love-child, she explained.
        And smiled, for our intelligence.

'Now, Gentlemen of the Jury,' said
        The coroner—'this woman's child
By misadventure met its death.'
        'Aye, aye,' said we. The mother smiled.

And I could see that child's one eye
        Which seemed to laugh, and say with glee:
'What caused my death you'll never know—
        Perhaps my mother murdered me.'

ONE POET VISITS ANOTHER

*W. H.
Davies*

His car was worth a thousand pounds and more,
A tall and glossy black silk hat he wore;
His clothes were pressed, like pretty leaves, when
        they
Are found in Bibles closed for many a day;
Until the birds I love dropped something that—
        As white as milk, but thick as any cream—
Went pit, pit, pat! Right on his lovely hat!
        .   .   .   .

Lead this unhappy poet to his car—
        Where is his longing now, where his desire?
When left alone, I'll ride him to his grave,
        On my own little horse of wind and fire.

THE POET

W. H.
Davies

When I went down past Charing Cross,
    A plain and simple man was I;
I might have been no more than air,
    Unseen by any mortal eye.

But, Lord in Heaven, had I the power
    To show my inward spirit there,
Then what a pack of human hounds
    Had hunted me, to strip me bare.

A human pack, ten thousand strong,
    All in full cry to bring me down;
All greedy for my magic robe,
    All crazy for my burning crown.

Walter
le la Mare

THE BARDS

My aged friend, Miss Wilkinson,
    Whose mother was a Lambe,
Saw Wordsworth once, and Coleridge, too,
    One morning in her p'ram'.

Birdlike the bards stooped over her—
    Like fledgling in a nest:
And Wordsworth said: 'Thou harmless babe!'
    And Coleridge was impressed.

[52]

The pretty thing gazed up and smiled,
    And softly murmured, 'Coo!'
William was then aged sixty-four
    And Samuel sixty-two.

BUTTONS

*Walter
de la Mare*

There was an old skinflint of Hitching
Had a cook, Mrs Casey, of Cork;
There was nothing but crusts in the kitchen,
    While in parlour was sherry and pork.
So at last, Mrs Casey, her pangs to assuage,
Having snipped off his buttonses, curried the page;
And now, while that skinflint gulps sherry and pork
    In his parlour adjacent to Hitching,
To the tune blithe and merry of knife and of fork,
    Anthropophagy reigns in the kitchen.

AT THE KEYHOLE

*Walter
de la Mare*

'Grill me some bones,' said the Cobbler,
    'Some bones, my pretty Sue;
I'm tired of my lonesome with heels and soles,
Springsides and uppers too;

[53]

A mouse in the wainscot is nibbling;
A wind in the keyhole drones;
And a sheet webbed over my candle, Susie,—
    Grill me some bones!

'Grill me some bones,' said the Cobbler,
    'I sat at my tic-tac-to;
And a footstep came to my door and stopped,
And a hand groped to and fro;
And I peered up over my boot and last;
And my feet went cold as stones:—
I saw an eye at the keyhole, Susie!—
    Grill me some bones!'

Lawrence Durrell

MYTHOLOGY

All my favourite characters have been
Out of all pattern and proportion:
Some living in villas by railways,
Some like Katsimbalis heard but seldom seen,
And others in banks whose sunless hands
Moved like great rats on ledgers.

Tibble, Gondril, Purvis, the Duke of Puke,
Shatterblossom and Dude Bowdler
Who swelled up in Jaffa and became a tree:
Hollis who had wives killed under him like horses
And that man of destiny,

[54]

Ramon de Something who gave lectures
From an elephant founded a society
To protect the inanimate against cruelty.
He gave asylum to aged chairs in his home,
Lampposts and crockery, everything that
Seemed to him suffering he took in
Without mockery.

The poetry was in the pity. No judgment
Disturbs people like these in their frames
O men of the Marmion class, sons of the free.

THE GROUNDHOG

*Richard
Eberhart*

In June, amid the golden fields,
I saw a groundhog lying dead.
Dead lay he; my senses shook,
And mind outshot our naked frailty.
There lowly in the vigorous summer
His form began its senseless change,
And made my senses waver dim
Seeing nature ferocious in him.
Inspecting close his maggots' might
And seething cauldron of his being,
Half with loathing, half with a strange love,
I poked him with an angry stick.

[55]

The fever arose, became a frame
And Vigour circumscribed the skies,
Immense energy in the sun,
And through my frame a sunless trembling.
My stick had done nor good nor harm.
Then stood I silent in the day
Watching the object, as before;
And kept my reverence for knowledge
Trying for control, to be still,
To quell the passion of the blood;
Until I had bent down on my knees
Praying for joy in the sight of decay.
And so I left; and I returned
In Autumn strict of eye, to see
The sap gone out of the groundhog,
But the bony sodden hulk remained.
But the year had lost its meaning,
And in intellectual chains
I lost both love and loathing,
Mured up in the wall of wisdom.
Another summer took the fields again
Massive and burning, full of life,
But when I chanced upon the spot
There was only a little hair left,
And bones bleaching in the sunlight
Beautiful as architecture;
I watched them like a geometer,
And cut a walking stick from a birch.
It has been three years, now.
There is no sign of the groundhog.
I stood there in the whirling summer,

My hand capped a withered heart,
And thought of China and of Greece,
Of Alexander in his tent;
Of Montaigne in his tower,
Of Saint Theresa in her wild lament.

JOURNEY OF THE MAGI

T. S.
Eliot

'A cold coming we had of it,
Just the worst time of the year
For a journey, and such a long journey:
The ways deep and the weather sharp,
The very dead of winter.'
And the camels galled, sore-footed, refractory,
Lying down in the melting snow.
There were times we regretted
The summer palaces on slopes, the terraces,
And the silken girls bringing sherbet.
Then the camel men cursing and grumbling
And running away, and wanting their liquor and
    women,
And the night-fires going out, and the lack of shelters,
And the cities hostile and the towns unfriendly
And the villages dirty and charging high prices:
A hard time we had of it.
At the end we preferred to travel all night,
Sleeping in snatches,
With the voices singing in our ears, saying
That this was all folly.

Then at dawn we came down to a temperate valley,
Wet, below the snow line, smelling of vegetation;
With a running stream and a water-mill beating the
    darkness,
And three trees on the low sky,
And an old white horse galloped away in the meadow.
Then we came to a tavern with vine-leaves over the
    lintel,
Six hands at an open door dicing for pieces of silver,
And feet kicking the empty wine-skins.
But there was no information, and so we continued
And arrived at evening, not a moment too soon
Finding the place; it was (you may say) satisfactory.

All this was a long time ago, I remember,
And I would do it again, but set down
This set down
This: were we led all that way for
Birth or Death? There was a Birth, certainly,
We had evidence and no doubt. I had seen birth
    and death,
But had thought they were different; this Birth was
Hard and bitter agony for us, like Death, our death.
We returned to our places, these Kingdoms,
But no longer at ease here, in the old dispensation,
With an alien people clutching their gods.
I should be glad of another death.

RAFTERY'S DIALOGUE WITH THE WHISKEY

RAFTERY

If you shortened many a road and put a halo
On every thought that was growing in my head,
Have I not been to you as the brown nut to the hazel,
Your fruit, O my comrade?
And in many a lonely bed have I not praised you
With sleepy words no virgin ever heard?
And after all this, O the spite of it, here in Kilchreest
You topple a tallow candle and burn my beard.

Troy in its tall sticks never burned with a blaze
As bright as Raftery's hairs when that evil spark
Leaped on his skull and from that holy rooftree
Pitchforked his spluttering thatch;
Shame on you! not even Mercury who rose
Out of the cradle to fall on evil ways,
Stealing cattle, would hobble my wits and roast them
Hide and hair like that in the fire of my face.

O I was the sight then and the great commotion;
Wells running dry and poor people peeling their legs
With barrels and pails, and the fish flying down to
    the ocean;
And look at me now! a mere plaster of white of eggs!
Look at me! a bonfire to folly! but no man
Was ever saint till he was a sinner first;
And I'll break with you now though it cost me the
    mannerly company
Of the gay talkers who follow a thirst.

*Padraic
Fallon*

[59]

So I dismiss you. Here! Take your mouth from my
  mouth!
I have weighed you, O creature of air, and the weigh-
  man cries,
'Here's nothing will balance a holding of land in the
  south,
Beef on the hoof there and grass climbing up to the
  skies;
What's whiskey to hanging bacon?
To a glittering hearth and blue delphware?
Will it put a Sunday coat on any man,
I ask you, or leave him to walk bare?'

Ah, sweet whisperer, my dear wanton, I
Have followed you, shawled in your warmth, since I
  left the breast,
Been toady for you and pet bully,
And a woeful heartscald to the parish priest;
And look! If I took the mint by storm and spent it,
Heaping on you in one wild night the dazzle of a
  king's whore,
And returned next morning with no money for a
  curer,
Your Publican would throw me out of the door.

  THE WHISKEY
You blow hot and cold, grumbling,
The privilege of the woman and the poet.
Now let me advise you, Man of the fancy stomach,
Carry a can and milk a nanny goat!

Drink milk! for I am not for you—as I am not
    indeed
For your brother the miser; but, ah, when the miser's
    heir
Grows into manhood and squanders I'll walk through
    the company
And call that man my dear.

I grow too heady now for your grey blood;
And you do little good to my reputation
With your knock-knees and tremulous jowls—for
    God's sake
Pay the tailor to press your pelt and tuck it in!
What can I be to you now but a young wife to an
    old man?
Leave me to the roarers in the great universities,
The masters of Latin with the big ferules
Who know what use strong whiskey is!

Hush, now! I'll speak or burst. You have no pith,
And I pity the botch of a carpenter who planed you
    down.
You are maudlin at table ere the company is lit,
And among clowns, the heaviest clown.
I have given you pleasure, yet you round on me like
    a lackey
Who will swear he was overworked and underpaid;
And tomorrow, O most grievous insult of all, you'll
    repent of me
That the priest may help you into a holy grave.

RAFTERY

Ah, that tongue was sharpened in many a bad house
Where candles are hooded on the black quays of the
    world;
Many is the sailor it stripped to the bleak hose
And the Light Dragoon with his feather furled;
I hear it now and I pray that a great bishop
Will rise with a golden crook and rout you out of the
    land,
Yourself and the rising family of your sins,
As Patrick drove the worms out of Ireland.

You're an illness, a cancer, canker, a poison,
Galloping consumption, broken breath,
Indiaman's liver, thin diseases of the person,
Cholera Morbus and the yellow death;
You're the two sour women who wait here by my
    mattress
With Christian charity and broken hen-eggs
To mess my only features, but if I live to denounce
    you
I'll empty every tavern when I get upon my legs.

THE WHISKEY

If hard words broke bones every sad rascal
With a bleached tongue who turns on me of a
    morning
Would have done for me long ago, yet I rise again
    like the pasch
Quietly, brightly, in their minds and they return.

[62]

RAFTERY

Who returns but the shiftless drifters, the moon's
    men?
Stray calves who'd suck at any udder?
Waifs, bagmen, beggars, and an odd fool of a lord
Crazy enough not to know better?

THE WHISKEY

Men of merriment, the wide girthed men
Whose eyes pen cattle, and slender men who hold
The curves of a filly together with one finger
While the other strips an heiress of her gold;
Equal those, O Fiddler, men of the great gay world
Who can dance a stately figure or bow prettily to a
    queen
And keep fine manners though the blood be rearing
Like a red stallion on the fair green.

RAFTERY

Blackguards, rakes, who rise up from cards
Only when the sun is trumped there on the table
Like the red ace of hearts, take them, the gamblers
Who wouldn't pay their debts were they able;
Dicers, procurers, who'll give you an I.O.U.
On the honour or dishonour of a wife or daughter,
Take them, the lot of them, hog, devil, or dog,
And drown them in a bucket of bog water.

THE WHISKEY

Poets and musicians——

RAFTERY

and absentee landlords,
Militiamen on hayfeet—strawfeet who burn
Brightly as red lamps in a lanewife's back parlour,
Taking, as always, the wrong turn;
I leave you to them and to the landlord's agent
Who shivers beside you day-in day-out
Walled in by the hostile murmurs of the rainy grass-
    lands
In an old windy house.

THE WHISKEY
For a homespun poet whose pride I nursed
When doors were shut on him and dogs barked at his
    heels,
Your gratitude is such I'll swear a cutpurse was your
    father
And your mother the lady who tied eels.
Desert me, indeed? You windy bag of old words,
You wan wizened weasel with one worn tooth!
If I whistled tomorrow you'd hobble to me on your
    sores;
And that's the truth.

RAFTERY
Whistle, then!

THE WHISKEY
                    I'll whistle when
I'm in the mood.

RAFTERY
Whistle! Whistle!

THE WHISKEY
Maybe when you've money and can spend,
When you're a farmer slaughtering the poor thistle,
Stoning crows or coaxing cows,
Counting your corn grain by grain,
With thirteen bonhams to every one of your sows,
And you carrying a big purse at the fair.

RAFTERY
Good-bye for ever then!

THE WHISKEY
                    Good-bye Raftery.

RAFTERY
I'll never be a farmer.

THE WHISKEY
                              And where is the need?
Poetry and whiskey have lived always on the country.
Why wouldn't they indeed?

RAFTERY
You're right. Why shouldn't I tax the heavy farmer?
I give him wit. And you? You give him—what?

[65]

THE WHISKEY
No matter. We are two necessary luxuries.

RAFTERY
Listen! I'll drink to that.

*Oliver
St John
Gogarty*

O BOYS! O BOYS!

O Boys, the times I've seen!
The things I've done and known!
If you knew where I have been,
Or half the joys I've had,
You never would leave me alone;
But pester me to tell,
Swearing to keep it dark,
What . . . but I know quite well:
Every solicitor's clerk
Would break out and go mad;
And all the dogs would bark!

There was a young fellow of old
Who spoke of a wonderful town,
Built on a lake of gold,
With many a barge and raft
Afloat in the cooling sun,
And lutes upon the lake
Played by such courtesans . . .

The sight was enough to take
The reason out of a man's
Brain; and to leave him daft,
Babbling of lutes and fans.

The tale was right enough:
Willows and orioles,
And ladies skilled in love:
But they listened only to smirk,
For he spoke to incredulous fools,
And, maybe, was sorry he spoke;
For no one believes in joys,
And Peace on Earth is a joke,
Which, anyhow, telling destroys;
So better go on with your work:
But Boys! O Boys! O Boys!

OPPORTUNITY

Harry
Graham

When Mrs Gorm (Aunt Eloïse)
Was stung to death by savage bees,
Her husband (Prebendary Gorm)
Put on his veil, and took the swarm.
He's publishing a book, next May,
On 'How to Make Bee-keeping Pay.'

THE BARDS

*Robert
Graves*

Their cheeks are blotched for shame, their running
    verse
Stumbles, with marrow-bones the drunken diners
Pelt them as they delay:
It is a something fearful in the song
Plagues them, an unknown grief that like a churl
Goes commonplace in cowskin
And bursts unheralded, crowing and coughing,
An unpilled holly-club twirled in his hand,
Into their many-shielded, samite-curtained
Jewel-bright hall where twelve kings sit at chess
Over the white-bronze pieces and the gold,
And by a gross enchantment
Flails down the rafters and leads off the queens—
The wild-swan-breasted, the rose-ruddy-cheeked
Raven-haired daughters of their admiration—
To stir his black pots and to bed on straw.

*Robert
Graves*

LOLLOCKS

By sloth on sorrow fathered,
These dusty-featured Lollocks
Have their nativity in all disordered
Backs of cupboard drawers.

They play hide and seek
Among collars and novels

And empty medicine bottles,
And letters from abroad
That never will be answered.

Every sultry night
They plague little children,
Gurgling from the cistern,
Humming from the air,
Skewing up the bed-clothes,
Twitching the blind.

When the imbecile agèd
Are over-long in dying
And the nurse drowses,
Lollocks come skipping
Up the tattered stairs
And are nasty together
In the bed's shadow.

The signs of their presence
Are boils on the neck,
Dreams of vexation suddenly recalled
In the middle of the morning,
Languor after food.

Men cannot see them,
Men cannot hear them,
Do not believe in them—
But suffer the more,
Both in neck and belly.

[69]

Women can see them—
O those naughty wives
Who sit by the fireside
Munching bread and honey,
Watching them in mischief
From corners of their eyes,
Slyly allowing them to lick
Honey-sticky fingers.

Sovereign against Lollocks
Are hard broom and soft broom,
To well comb the hair,
To well brush the shoe,
And to pay every debt
As it falls due.

SONG: LIFT BOY

Robert
Graves

Let me tell you the story of how I began:
I began as the knife-boy and ended as the boot-man,
With nothing in my pockets but a jack-knife and a
    button,
With nothing in my pockets but a jack-knife and a
    button,
With nothing in my pockets.

Let me tell you the story of how I went on:
I began as the lift-boy and ended as the lift-man,
With nothing in my pockets but a jack-knife and a
    button,

With nothing in my pockets but a jack-knife and a
     button,
With nothing in my pockets.

I found it very easy to whistle and play
With nothing in my head or my pockets all day,
With nothing in my pockets.

But along came Old Eagle, like Moses or David,
He stopped at the fourth floor and preached me
     Damnation:
'Not a soul shall be savèd, not one shall be savèd.
The whole First Creation shall forfeit salvation:
From knife-boy to lift-boy, from ragged to regal,
Not one shall be savèd, not you, not Old Eagle,
No soul on earth escapeth, even if all repent——'
So I cut the cords of the lift and down we went,
With nothing in our pockets.

GROTESQUE

Sir John addressed the Snake-god in his temple,
Which was full of bats, not as a votary
But with the somewhat cynical courtesy,
Just short of condescension,
He might have paid the Governor-General
Of a small, hot, backward colony.
He was well versed in primitive religion,
But found this an embarrassing occasion:
The God was immense, noisy and affable,

*Robert
Graves*

Began to tickle him with a nervous chuckle,
Unfobbed a great gold clock for him to listen,
Hissed like a snake, and swallowed him at one
    mouthful.

Robert
Graves

GROTESQUE

Dr Newman with the crooked pince-nez
Had studied in Vienna and Chicago.
Chess was his only relaxation.
And Dr Newman remained unperturbed
By every nastier manifestation
Of pluto-democratic civilization:
All that was cranky, corny, ill-behaved,
Unnecessary, askew or orgiastic
Would creep unbidden to his side-door (hidden
Behind a poster in the Tube Station,
Nearly half-way up the moving stairs),
Push its way in, to squat there undisturbed
Among box-files and tubular-steel chairs.
He was once seen at the Philharmonic Hall
Noting the reactions of two patients,
With pronounced paranoiac tendencies,
To old Dutch music. He appeared to recall
A tin of lozenges in his breast-pocket,
Put his hand confidently in—
And drew out a black imp, or sooterkin,
Six inches long, with one ear upside-down,
Licking at a vanilla ice-cream cornet—
Then put it back again with a slight frown.

COUNTING THE BEATS

You, love, and I,
(He whispers) you and I,
And if no more than only you and I
What care you or I?

*Robert
Graves*

Counting the beats,
Counting the slow heart beats,
The bleeding to death of time in slow heart beats,
Wakeful they lie.

Cloudless day,
Night, and a cloudless day,
Yet the huge storm will burst upon their heads one
    day
From a bitter sky.

Where shall we be,
(She whispers) where shall we be,
When death strikes home, O where then shall we be
Who were you and I?

Not there but here,
(He whispers) only here,
As we are, here, together, now and here,
Always you and I.

Counting the beats,
Counting the slow heart beats,
The bleeding to death of time in slow heart beats,
Wakeful they lie.

[73]

TRAVELLER'S CURSE AFTER MISDIRECTION

From the Welsh

*Robert
Graves*

May they stumble, stage by stage
On an endless pilgrimage,
Dawn and dusk, mile after mile,
At each and every step, a stile;
At each and every step withal
May they catch their feet and fall;
At each and every fall they take
May a bone within them break;
And may the bone that breaks within
Not be, for variation's sake
Now rib, now thigh, now arm, now shin,
But always, without fail, THE NECK.

*Robert
Graves*

THE GREAT-GRANDMOTHER

That aged woman with the bass voice
And yellowing white hair: believe her.
Though to your grandfather, her son, she lied
And to your father disingenuously
Told half the tale as the whole,
Yet she was honest with herself,
Knew disclosure was not yet due,
Knows it is due now.

She will conceal nothing of consequence
From you, her great-grandchildren

[74]

(So distant the relationship,
So near her term),
Will tell you frankly, she has waited
Only for your sincere indifference
To exorcise that filial regard
Which has estranged her, seventy years,
From the folk of her house.

Confessions of old distaste
For music, sighs and roses—
Their false-innocence assaulting her,
Breaching her hard heart;
Of the pleasures of a full purse,
Of clean brass and clean linen,
Of being alone at last:
Disgust with the ailing poor
To whom she was bountiful;
How the prattle of young children
Vexed more than if they whined;
How she preferred cats.

She will say, yes, she acted well,
Took such pride in the art
That none of them suspected, even,
Her wrathful irony
In doing what they asked
Better than they could ask it. . . .
But, ah, how grudgingly her will returned
After the severance of each navel-cord,
And fled how far again,
When again she was kind!

She has outlasted all man-uses,
As was her first resolve:
Happy and idle like a port
After the sea's recession,
She does not misconceive the nature
Of shipmen or of ships.
Hear her, therefore, as the latest voice;
The intervening generations (drifting
On tides of fancy still), ignore.

THE OLDEST SOLDIER

Robert Graves

The sun shines warm on seven old soldiers
    Paraded in a row,
Perched like starlings on the railings—
    Give them plug-tobacco!

They'll croon you the Oldest-Soldier Song:
    Of Harry who took a holiday
From the sweat of ever thinking for himself
    Or going his own bloody way.

It was arms-drill, guard and kit-inspection,
    Like dreams of a long train-journey,
And the barrack-bed that Harry dossed on
    Went rockabye, rockabye, rockabye.

Harry kept his rifle and brasses clean,
    But Jesus Christ, what a liar!
He won the Military Medal
    For his coolness under fire.

He was never the last on parade
    Nor the first to volunteer,
And when Harry rose to be storeman
    He seldom had to pay for his beer.

Twenty-one years, and out Harry came
    To be odd-job man, or janitor,
Or commissionaire at a picture-house,
    Or, some say, bully to a whore.

But his King and Country calling Harry,
    He reported again at the Depôt,
To perch on this railing like a starling,
    The oldest soldier of the row.

TO LIZBIE BROWNE
*Thomas
Hardy*

Dear Lizbie Browne,
Where are you now?
In sun, in rain?—
Or is your brow
Past joy, past pain,
Dear Lizbie Browne?

Sweet Lizbie Browne,
How you could smile,
How you could sing!—
How archly wile
In glance-giving,
Sweet Lizbie Browne!

[77]

And, Lizbie Browne,
Who else had hair
Bay-red as yours,
Or flesh so fair
Bred out of doors,
Sweet Lizbie Browne?

When, Lizbie Browne,
You had just begun
To be endeared
By stealth to one,
You disappeared
My Lizbie Browne!

Ay, Lizbie Browne,
So swift your life,
And mine so slow,
You were a wife
Ere I could show
Love, Lizbie Browne.

Still, Lizbie Browne,
You won, they said,
The best of men
When you were wed.
Where went you then,
O Lizbie Browne?

Dear Lizbie Browne,
I should have thought,
'Girls ripen fast,'

And coaxed and caught
You ere you passed,
Dear Lizbie Browne!

But, Lizbie Browne,
I let you slip;
Shaped not a sign;
Touched never your lip
With lip of mine,
Lost Lizbie Browne!

So, Lizbie Browne,
When on a day
Men speak of me
As not, you'll say,
'And who was he?'—
Yes, Lizbie Browne!

AT CASTLE BOTEREL

Thomas Hardy

As I drive to the junction of lane and highway,
  And the drizzle bedrenches the waggonette,
I look behind at the fading byway,
  And see on its slope, now glistening wet,
    Distinctly yet

Myself and a girlish form benighted
  In dry March weather. We climb the road
Beside a chaise. We had just alighted
  To ease the sturdy pony's load
    When he sighed and slowed.

What we did as we climbed, and what we talked of
    Matters not much, nor to what it led,—
Something that life will not be balked of
    Without rude reason till hope is dead,
        And feeling fled.

It filled but a minute. But was there ever
    A time of such quality, since or before,
In that hill's story? To one mind never,
    Though it has been climbed, foot-swift, foot-sore,
        By thousands more.

Primaeval rocks form the road's steep border,
    And much have they faced there, first and last,
Of the transitory in Earth's long order;
    But what they record in colour and cast
        Is—that we two passed.

And to me, though Time's unflinching rigour,
    In mindless rote, has ruled from sight
The substance now, one phantom figure
    Remains on the slope, as when that night
        Saw us alight.

I look and see it there, shrinking, shrinking,
    I look back at it amid the rain
For the very last time; for my sand is sinking,
    And I shall traverse old love's domain
        Never again.

I NEED NOT GO

Thomas Hardy

I need not go
Through sleet and snow
To where I know
She waits for me;
She will tarry me there
Till I find it fair,
And have time to spare
From company.

When I've overgot
The world somewhat,
When things cost not
Such stress and strain,
Is soon enough
By cypress sough
To tell my Love
I am come again.

And if some day,
When none cries nay,
I still delay
To seek her side,
(Though ample measure
Of fitting leisure
Await my pleasure)
She will not chide.

What—not upbraid me
That I delayed me,

Nor ask what stayed me
So long? Ah, no!—
New cares may claim me,
New loves inflame me,
She will not blame me,
But suffer it so.

IN DEATH DIVIDED

*Thomas
Hardy*

I shall rot here, with those whom in their day
    You never knew,
And alien ones who, ere they chilled to clay,
    Met not my view,
Will in your distant grave-place ever neighbour you.

No shade of pinnacle or tree or tower,
    While earth endures,
Will fall on my mound and within the hour
    Steal on to yours;
One robin never haunt our two green covertures.

Some organ may resound on Sunday noons
    By where you lie,
Some other thrill the panes with other tunes
    Where moulder I;
No selfsame chords compose our common lullaby.

The simply-cut memorial at my head
    Perhaps may take
A rustic form, and that above your bed
    A stately make;
No linking symbol show thereon for our tale's sake.

And in the monotonous moils of strained, hard-run
    Humanity,
The eternal tie which binds us twain in one
    No eye will see
Stretching across the miles that sever you from me.

AFTER A JOURNEY

*Thomas
Hardy*

Hereto I come to view a voiceless ghost;
    Whither, O whither will its whim now draw me?
Up the cliff, down, till I'm lonely, lost,
    And the unseen waters' ejaculations awe me.
Where you will next be there's no knowing,
    Facing round about me everywhere,
      With your nut-coloured hair,
And gray eyes, and rose-flush coming and going.

Yes: I have re-entered your olden haunts at last;
    Through the years, through the dead scenes I have
      tracked you;
What have you now found to say of our past—
    Scanned across the dark space wherein I have
      lacked you?

Summer gave us sweets, but autumn wrought divi-
    sion?
  Things were not lastly as firstly well
    With us twain, you tell?
But all's closed now, despite Time's derision.

I see what you are doing: you are leading me on
  To the spots we knew when we haunted here
    together,
The waterfall, above which the mist-bow shone
  At the then fair hour in the then fair weather,
And the cave just under, with a voice still so hollow
  That it seems to call out to me from forty years ago,
    When you were all aglow,
And not the thin ghost that I now frailly follow!

Ignorant of what there is flitting here to see,
  The waked birds preen and the seals flop lazily,
Soon you will have, Dear, to vanish from me,
  For the stars close their shutters and the dawn
    whitens hazily.
Trust me, I mind not, though Life lours,
  The bringing me here; nay, bring me here again!
    I am just the same as when
Our days were a joy, and our paths through flowers.

A BROKEN APPOINTMENT

You did not come,
And marching Time drew on and wore me numb.—
Yet less for loss of your dear presence there
Than that I thus found lacking in your make
That high compassion which can overbear
Reluctance for pure lovingkindness' sake
Grieved I, when, as the hope-hour stroked its sum,
    You did not come.

You love not me,
And love alone can lend you loyalty;
—I know and knew it. But, unto the store
Of human deeds divine in all but name,
Was it not worth a little hour or more
To add yet this: Once, you, a woman, came
To soothe a time-torn man; even though it be
    You love not me?

*Thomas
Hardy*

THE CHOIRMASTER'S BURIAL

*Thomas
Hardy*

He often would ask us
That, when he died,
After playing so many
To their last rest,
If out of us any
Should here abide,
And it would not task us,
We would with our lutes

[85]

Play over him
By his grave-brim
The psalm he liked best—
The one whose sense suits
'Mount Ephraim'—
And perhaps we should seem
To him, in Death's dream,
Like the seraphim.

As soon as I knew
That his spirit was gone
I thought this his due,
And spoke thereupon.
'I think', said the vicar,
'A read service quicker
Than viols out-of-doors
In these frosts and hoars.
That old-fashioned way
Requires a fine day,
And it seems to me
It had better not be.'

Hence, that afternoon,
Though never knew he
That his wish could not be,
To get through it faster
They buried the master
Without any tune.

But 'twas said that, when
At the dead of next night

The vicar looked out,
There struck on his ken
Thronged roundabout,
Where the frost was graying
The headstoned grass,
A band all in white
Like the saints in church-glass,
Singing and playing
The ancient stave
By the choirmaster's grave.

Such the tenor man told
When he had grown old.

IN CHURCH

*Thomas
Hardy*

'And now to God the Father,' he ends,
And his voice thrills up to the topmost tiles:
Each listener chokes as he bows and bends,
And emotion pervades the crowded aisles.
Then the preacher glides to the vestry-door,
And shuts it, and thinks he is seen no more.

The door swings softly ajar meanwhile,
And a pupil of his in the Bible class,
Who adores him as one without gloss or guile,
Sees her idol stand with a satisfied smile
And re-enact at the vestry-glass
Each pulpit gesture in deft dumb-show
That had moved the congregation so.

PRAYER

George Herbert

Prayer, the Churche's banquet, Angels' age,
   God's breath in man returning to his birth,
   The soul in paraphrase, heart in pilgrimage,
The Christian plummet sounding heav'n and earth;
Engine against th' Almightie, sinner's towre,
   Reversèd thunder, Christ-side-piercing spear,
   The six-daies-world transposing in an houre,
A kinde of tune which all things heare and fear;
Softnesse, and peace, and joy, and love, and blisse,
   Exalted manna, gladnesse of the best,
   Heaven in ordinarie, man well drest,
The milkie way, the bird of Paradise,
   Church-bels beyond the stars heard, the soul's
     bloud,
   The land of spices, something understood.

Robert Herrick

HIS LITANY TO THE HOLY SPIRIT

In the hour of my distress,
When temptations me oppress,
And when I my sins confess,
   Sweet Spirit, comfort me!

When I lie within my bed,
Sick in heart and sick in head,
And with doubts discomforted,
   Sweet Spirit, comfort me!

[88]

When the house doth sigh and weep,
And the world is drowned in sleep,
Yet mine eyes the watch do keep,
  Sweet Spirit, comfort me!

When the artless doctor sees
No one hope, but of his fees,
And his skill runs on the lees;
  Sweet Spirit, comfort me!

When his potion and his pill,
His, or none, or little skill,
Meet for nothing, but to kill;
  Sweet Spirit, comfort me!

When the passing bell doth toll,
And the Furies in a shoal
Come to fright a parting soul;
  Sweet Spirit, comfort me!

When the tapers now burn blue,
And the comforters are few,
And that number more than true;
  Sweet Spirit, comfort me!

When the priest his last hath prayed,
And I nod to what is said,
'Cause my speech is now decayed,
  Sweet Spirit, comfort me!

When, God knows, I'm toss'd about,
Either with despair or doubt;
Yet before the glass be out,
  Sweet Spirit, comfort me!

When the tempter me pursu'th
With the sins of all my youth,
And half damns me with untruth;
  Sweet Spirit, comfort me!

When the flames and hellish cries
Fright mine ears, and fright mine eyes,
And all terrors me surprise;
  Sweet Spirit, comfort me!

When the Judgment is revealed,
And that opened which was sealed,
When to Thee I have appealed;
  Sweet Spirit, comfort me!

*Thomas
Hood*

SHE IS FAR FROM THE LAND

Cables entangling her,
Shipspars for mangling her,
Ropes, sure of strangling her;
Blocks over-dangling her;
Tiller to batter her,
Topmast to shatter her,
Tobacco to spatter her;
Boreas blustering,

Boatswain quite flustering,
Thunder clouds mustering
To blast her with sulphur—
If the deep don't engulph her;
Sometimes fear's scrutiny
Pries out a mutiny,
Sniffs conflagration,
Or hints at starvation:—
All the sea-dangers,
Buccaneers, rangers,
Pirates, and Sallee-men,
Algerine galleymen,
Tornadoes and typhons,
And horrible syphons,
And submarine travels
Thro' roaring sea-navels;
Every thing wrong enough,
Long boat not long enough,
Vessels not strong enough;
Pitch marring frippery,
The deck very slippery,
And the cabin—built sloping,
The Captain a-toping,
And the Mate a blasphemer,
That names his Redeemer,—
With inward uneasiness;
The cook, known by greasiness,
The victuals beslubber'd,
Her bed—in a cupboard;
Things of strange christening,
Snatch'd in her listening,

[91]

Blue lights and red lights
And mention of dead lights,
And shrouds made a theme of,
Things horrid to dream of,—
And *buoys* in the water
To fear all exhort her;
Her friend no Leander,
Herself no sea gander,
And ne'er a cork jacket
On board of the packet;
The breeze still a stiffening,
The trumpet quite deafening;
Thoughts of repentance,
And doomsday and sentence;
Everything sinister,
Not a church minister,—
Pilot a blunderer,
Coral reefs under her,
Ready to sunder her;
Trunks tipsy-topsy,
The ship in a dropsy;
Waves oversurging her,
Syrens a-dirgeing her;
Sharks all expecting her,
Sword-fish dissecting her,
Crabs with their hand-vices:
Punishing land vices:
Sea-dogs and unicorns,
Things with no puny horns,
Mermen carnivorous—
'Good Lord deliver us!'

THE LEADEN ECHO AND
THE GOLDEN ECHO

Maidens' song from St Winefred's Well

Gerard
Manley
Hopkins

THE LEADEN ECHO

How to kéep—is there ány any, is there none such,
    nowhere known some, bow or brooch or braid or
    brace, láce, latch or catch or key to keep
Back beauty, keep it, beauty, beauty, beauty, . . . from
    vanishing away?
Ó is there no frowning of these wrinkles, rankèd
    wrinkles deep,
Dówn? no waving off of these most mournful
    messengers, still messengers, sad and stealing
    messengers of grey?
No there's none there's none, O no there's none,
Nor can you long be, what you now are, called fair,
Do what you may do, what, do what you may,
And wisdom is early to despair:
Be beginning; since, no, nothing can be done
To keep at bay
Age and age's evils, hoar hair,
Ruck and wrinkle, drooping, dying, death's worst,
    winding sheets, tombs and worms and tumbling to
    decay;
So be beginning, be beginning to despair.
O there's none; no no no there's none:
Be beginning to despair, to despair,
Despair, despair, despair, despair.

THE GOLDEN ECHO

Spare!

Gerard
Manley
Hopkins

There ís one, yes I have one (Hush there!);
Only not within seeing of the sun,
Not within the singeing of the strong sun,
Tall sun's tingeing, or treacherous the tainting of the
    earth's air,
Somewhere elsewhere there is ah well where! one,
Óne. Yes I cán tell such a key, I dó know such a
    place,
Where whatever's prized and passes of us, everything
    that's fresh and fast flying of us, seems to us sweet
    of us and swiftly away with, done away with,
    undone,
Úndone, done with, soon done with, and yet dearly
    and dangerously sweet
Of us, the wimpled-water-dimpled, not-by-mourn-
    ing-matchèd face,
The flower of beauty, fleece of beauty, too too apt
    to, ah! to fleet,
Never fleets móre, fastened with the tenderest truth
To its own best being and its loveliness of youth: it
    is an everlastingness of, O it is an all youth!
Come then, your ways and airs and looks, locks,
    maiden gear, gallantry and gaiety and grace,
Winning ways, airs innocent, maiden manners, sweet
    looks, loose locks, long locks, lovelocks, gaygear,
    going gallant, girlgrace—
Resign them, sign them, seal them, send them, motion
    them with breath,

[94]

And with sighs soaring, soaring síghs deliver
Them; beauty-in-the-ghost, deliver it, early now,
    long before death
Give beauty back, beauty, beauty, beauty, back to
    God, beauty's self and beauty's giver.
See; not a hair is, not an eyelash, not the least lash
    lost; every hair
Is, hair of the head, numbered.
Nay, what we had lighthanded left in surly the mere
    mould
Will have waked and have waxed and have walked
    with the wind what while we slept,
This side, that side hurling a heavyheaded hundred-
    fold
What while we, while we slumbered.
O then, weary then whý should we tread? O why
    are we so haggard at the heart, so care-coiled,
    care-killed, so fagged, so fashed, so cogged, so
    cumbered,
When the thing we freely fórfeit is kept with fonder
    a care,
Fonder a care kept than we could have kept it, kept
Far with fonder a care (and we, we should have lost
    it) finer, fonder
A care kept—Where kept? Do but tell us where kept,
    where.—
Yonder.—What high as that! We follow, now we
    follow.—
    Yonder, yes yonder, yonder,
Yonder.

INFANT INNOCENCE

Alfred
Edward
Housman

The Grizzly Bear is huge and wild;
He has devoured the infant child.
The infant child is not aware
He has been eaten by the bear.

ESYLLT

Glyn
Jones

As he climbs down our hill, my kestrel rises,
Steering in silence up from five empty fields,
A smooth sun brushed brown across his shoulders,
Floating in wide circles, his warm wings stiff.
Their shadows cut; in new soft orange hunting boots
My lover crashes through the snapping bracken.

The still gorse-hissing hill burns, brags gold broom's
Outcropping quartz; each touched bush spills dew.
Strangely, last moment's parting was never sad,
But unreal, like my promised years; less felt
Than this intense and silver snail calligraphy
Scrawled here in the sun across these stones.

Why have I often wanted to cry out
More against his going when he has left my flesh
Only for the night? When he has gone out
Hot from my mother's kitchen, and my combs
Were on the table under the lamp, and the wind
Was banging the doors of the shed in the yard.

A CHRISTMAS CHILDHOOD (II)

My father played the melodion
Outside at our gate;
There were stars in the morning east
And they danced to his music.

*Patrick
Kavanagh*

Across the wild bogs his melodion called
To Lennons and Callans.
As I pulled on my trousers in a hurry
I knew some strange thing had happened.

Outside in the cow-house my mother
Made the music of milking;
The light of her stable-lamp was a star
And the frost of Bethlehem made it twinkle.

A water-hen screeched in the bog,
Mass-going feet
Crunched the wafer-ice on the pot-holes,
Somebody wistfully twisted the bellows wheel.

My child poet picked out the letters
On the grey stone,
In silver the wonder of a Christmas townland,
The winking glitter of a frosty dawn.

Cassiopeia was over
Cassidy's hanging hill,
I looked and three whin bushes rode across
The horizon—the Three Wise Kings.

An old man passing said:
'Can't he make it talk'—
The melodion. I hid in the doorway
And tightened the belt of my box-pleated coat.

I nicked six nicks on the door-post
With my penknife's big blade—
There was a little one for cutting tobacco.
And I was six Christmases of age.

My father played the melodion,
My mother milked the cows,
And I had a prayer like a white rose pinned
On the Virgin Mary's blouse.

Sidney   MOONLIGHT NIGHT ON THE PORT
Keyes

Some were unlucky. Blown a mile to shoreward.
Their crossed hands lie among the bitter marsh-
grass.

Link arms and sing. The moon sails out
Spreading distraction on the faces, drawing
The useful hands to birdclaws. . . .
                  If a ring
Flashes, what matter? Other hands are ringless.
We'll never go home to-night, never to-night.

And some shall be pulled down, revolving sickly
On the tide's whim, their bare feet scraping sand.

The moon is out, my lady; lady of different
Voices and gestures, with the same cold eyes.
The buoy swings ringing. Under the curved seawall
My hands reveal your soundings all the same.

Some were more gallant, dragged across the seabed
In iron cages, coughing out their lungs.

Singing in bars, running before the seven
Set winds of the heart; bearing our weakness bravely
Through all the frigid seasons, we have weighed
The chances against us, and refuse no kisses—
Even the tide's kiss on this dog-toothed shore.

For some are lucky, leaving their curved faces
Propped in the moonlight while their bodies drown.

END OF ANOTHER HOME HOLIDAY

*D. H.
Lawrence*

When shall I see the half-moon sink again
Behind the black sycamore at the end of the garden?
When will the scent of the dim white phlox
Creep up the wall to me, and in at my open window?

Why is it, the long, slow stroke of the midnight bell
    (Will it never finish the twelve?)
Falls again and again on my heart with a heavy
    reproach?

The moon-mist is over the village, out of the mist
    speaks the bell,
And all the little roofs of the village bow low, pitiful,
    beseeching, resigned.
—Speak, you my home! what is it I don't do well?

Ah home, suddenly I love you
As I hear the sharp clean trot of a pony down the
    road,
Succeeding sharp little sounds dropping into silence
Clear upon the long-drawn hoarseness of a train
    across the valley.

The light has gone out, from under my mother's
    door.
    That she should love me so!—
    She, so lonely, greying now!
    And I leaving her,
    Bent on my pursuits!

        Love is the great Asker.
        The sun and the rain do not ask the secret
        Of the time when the grain struggles down in
            the dark.
        The moon walks her lonely way without
            anguish,
        Because no-one grieves over her departure.

Forever, ever by my shoulder pitiful love will linger,
Crouching as little houses crouch under the mist
    when I turn.

Forever, out of the mist, the church lifts up a re-
proachful finger,
Pointing my eyes in wretched defiance where love
hides her face to mourn.
Oh! but the rain creeps down to wet the grain
That struggles alone in the dark,
And asking nothing, patiently steals back again!
The moon sets forth o'nights
To walk the lonely, dusky heights
Serenely, with steps unswerving;
Pursued by no sigh of bereavement,
No tears of love unnerving
Her constant tread:
While ever at my side,
Frail and sad, with grey, bowed head,
The beggar-woman, the yearning-eyed
Inexorable love goes lagging.

The wild young heifer, glancing distraught,
With a strange new knocking of life at her side
Runs seeking a loneliness.
The little grain draws down the earth, to hide.
Nay, even the slumberous egg, as it labours under
the shell
Patiently to divide and self-divide,
Asks to be hidden, and wishes nothing to tell.

But when I draw the scanty cloak of silence over my
eyes
Piteous love comes peering under the hood;

Touches the clasp with trembling fingers, and tries
To put her ear to the painful sob of my blood;
While her tears soak through to my breast,
    Where they burn and cauterize.

    The moon lies back and reddens.
    In the valley a corncrake calls
        Monotonously,
    With a plaintive, unalterable voice, that deadens
        My confident activity;
    With a hoarse, insistent request that falls
        Unweariedly, unweariedly,
        Asking something more of me,
            Yet more of me.

*D. H.
Lawrence*

SHIP OF DEATH

I sing of autumn and the falling fruit
and the long journey towards oblivion.

The apples falling like great drops of dew
to bruise themselves an exit from themselves.

Have you built your ship of death, oh, have you?
Build then your ship of death, for you will need it!

Can man his own quietus make
with a bare bodkin?

With daggers, bodkins, bullets, man can make
a bruise or break of exit for his life
but is that a quietus, oh tell me, is it quietus?

Quietus is the goal of the long journey
the longest journey towards oblivion.

Slips out the soul, invisible one, wrapped still
in the white shirt of the mind's experiences
and folded in the dark-red, unseen
mantle of the body's still mortal memories.

Frightened and alone, the soul slips out of the house
or is pushed out
to find himself on the crowded, arid margins of
    existence.
Oh, it is not so easy, I tell you it is not so easy
to set softly forth on the longest journey, the longest
    journey.

It is easy to be pushed out of the silvery city of the
    body
through any breach in the wall,
thrust out on to the grey grey beaches of shadow
the long marginal stretches of existence, crowded
    with lost souls
that intervene between our tower and the shaking sea
    of the beyond.

Oh build your ship of death, oh build it in time
and build it lovingly, and put it between the hands of
    your soul.

Once outside the gate of the walled silvery life of days
once outside, upon the grey marsh beaches, where
    lost souls moan

in millions, unable to depart
having no boat to launch upon the shaken, soundless
deepest and longest of seas,
once outside the gate
what will you do, if you have no ship of the soul?

Oh pity the dead that are dead, but cannot take
the journey, still they moan and beat
against the silvery adamant walls of this our exclusive
   existence.
They moan and beat, they gnash, they rage
they fall upon the new outcoming souls with rage
and they send arrows of anger, bullets and bombs of
   frustration
over the adamant walls of this, our by-no-means
   impregnable existence.

Pity, oh pity the poor dead that are only ousted from
   life
and crowd there on the grey mud beaches of the
   margins
gaunt and horrible
waiting, waiting till at last the ancient boatman with
   the common barge
shall take them aboard, towards the great goal of
   oblivion.

Pity the poor gaunt dead that cannot die
into the distance with receding oars
but must roam like outcast dogs on the margins of
   life,

and think of them, and with the soul's deep sigh
waft nearer to them the bark of delivery.

But for myself, but for my soul, dear soul
let me build a little ship with oars and food
and little dishes, and all accoutrements
dainty and ready for the departing soul.

And put it between the hands of the trembling soul.
So that when the hour comes, and the last door closes
   behind him
he shall slip down the shores invisible
between the half-visible hordes
to where the furthest and the longest sea
touches the margins of our life's existence
with wincing unwilling waves.

And launching there his little ship,
wrapped in the dark-red mantle of the body's
   memories
the little, slender soul sits swiftly down, and takes
   the oars
and draws away, away, away, towards the dark depths
fathomless deep ahead, far, far from the grey shores
that fringe with shadow all this world's existence.

Over the sea, over the farthest sea
on the longest journey
past the jutting rocks of shadow
past the lurking, octopus arms of agonised memory
past the strange whirlpools of remembered greed
through the dead weed of a life-time's falsity,

slow, slow my soul, in his little ship
on the most soundless of all seas
taking the longest journey.

Pulling the long oars of a life-time's courage
drinking the confident water from the little jug
and eating the brave bread of a wholesome know-
    ledge
row, little soul, row on
on the longest journey, towards the greatest goal.

Neither straight nor crooked, neither here nor there
but shadows folded on deeper shadows
and deeper, to a core of sheer oblivion
like the convolutions of shadow-shell
or deeper, like the foldings and involvings of a womb.

Drift on, drift on, my soul, towards the most pure
most dark oblivion.
And at the penultimate porches, the dark-red mantle
of the body's memories slips and is absorbed
into the shell-like, womb-like convoluted shadow.

And round the great final bend of unbroken dark
the skirt of the spirit's experience has melted away
the oars have gone from the boat, and the little dishes
gone, gone, and the boat dissolves like pearl
as the soul at last slips perfect into the goal, the core
of sheer oblivion and of utter peace,
the womb of silence in the living night.

Ah peace, ah lovely peace, most lovely lapsing
of this my soul into the plasm of peace.

Oh lovely last, last lapse of death, into pure oblivion
at the end of the longest journey
peace, complete peace!
But can it be that also it is procreation?

Oh build your ship of death
oh build it!
Oh, nothing matters but the longest journey.

IN HOSPITAL: POONA (I)

*Alun
Lewis*

Last night I did not fight for sleep
But lay awake from midnight while the world
Turned its slow features to the moving deep
Of darkness, till I knew that you were furled,

Beloved, in the same dark watch as I.
And sixty degrees of longitude beside
Vanished as though a swan in ecstasy
Had spanned the distance from your sleeping side.

And like to swan or moon the whole of Wales
Glided within the parish of my care:
I saw the green tide leap on Cardigan,
Your red yacht riding like a legend there,

And the great mountains, Dafydd and Llewelyn,
Plynlimmon, Cader Idris and Eryri
Threshing the darkness back from head and fin,
And also the small nameless mining valley

[107]

Whose slopes are scratched with streets and sprawl-
    ing graves
Dark in the lap of firwoods and great boulders
Where you lay waiting, listening to the waves—
My hot hands touched your white despondent
    shoulders

—And then ten thousand miles of daylight grew
Between us, and I heard the wild daws crake
In India's starving throat; whereat I knew
That Time upon the heart can break
But love survives the venom of the snake.

IN HOSPITAL: POONA (II)

Alun
Lewis

The sun has sucked and beat the encircling hills
Into gaunt skeletons; the sick men watch
Soft shadows warm those bones of rock,
And the barefooted peasants winding back,
Sad withered loins in hanging dirty folds,
Mute sweepings from the disappointed streets,
Old shrunken tribes the starving dusk enfolds.
The wind sweeps up the rifle range and blows
The Parsis' long white robes, there where they go
Under the wheeling kites, bearing a corpse
To the high tower that the vultures know.

And from the polished ward where men lie ill
Thought rubs clean through the frayed cloth of the
    will,

Piercing the slow estrangement of disease,
And breaks into a state of blinding light
Where Now is a salt pillar, still and white,
And there are no familiar words or features
Nor blood nor tears no joy nor living creatures,
A void where Pain demands no cheap release
But white and rigid freezes into peace,
And mind lies coiled within green icebound streams
And sheds the stippled scales of ancient dreams.

And by that Arctic silence overawed
The mind crawls wounded from the lidless God,
And breeds again the hope that has no food
But lives amongst the evil and the good,
Biding its time amongst the lives that fail
While darkness crowds its dark piratic sail.
Yet in the garden of the hospital
The moonlight spills and sings in a stone pool,
Allowing those who loiter to recall
That which the whiplash sun drove out of bounds—
The heart's calm voice that stills the baying hounds.

SONG

On seeing dead bodies floating off the Cape

*Alun
Lewis*

The first month of his absence
I was numb and sick
And where he'd left his promise
Life did not turn or kick.
The seed, the seed of love was sick.

The second month my eyes were sunk
In the darkness of despair,
And my bed was like a grave
And his ghost was lying there.
And my heart was sick with care.

The third month of his going
I thought I heard him say
'Our course deflected slightly
On the thirty-second day——'
The tempest blew his words away.

And he was lost among the waves,
His ship rolled helpless in the sea.
The fourth month of his voyage
He shouted grievously
'Beloved, do not think of me.'

The flying fish like kingfishers
Skim the sea's bewildered crests,
The whales blow steaming fountains,
The seagulls have no nests
Where my lover sways and rests.

We never thought to buy and sell
This life that blooms or withers in the leaf,
And I'll not stir, so he sleeps well,
Though cell by cell the coral reef
Builds an eternity of grief.

But oh! the drag and dullness of my Self;
The turning seasons wither in my head;
All this slowness, all this hardness,
The nearness that is waiting in my bed,
The gradual self-effacement of the dead.

SACCO WRITES TO HIS SON

Alun
Lewis

I did not want to die. I wanted you,
You and your sister Inez and your mother.
Reject this death, my Dante, seek out Life,
Yet not the death-in-life that most men live.
My body aches . . . I think I hear you weep.
You must not weep. Tears are a waste of strength.
Seven years your mother wept, not as your mother,
But as my wife. So make her more your mother.
Take her the ways I know she can escape
From the poor soulness that so wearies her.
Take her into the country every Sunday,
Ask her the name of such and such a plant,
Gather a basket each of herbs and flowers,
Ask her to find the robin where he nests,
She will be happy then. Tears do no damage
That spring from gladness, though they scald the
    throat.
Go patiently about it. Not too much
Just yet, Dante, good boy. You'll know.

And for yourself, remember in the play
Of happiness you must not act alone.
The joy is in the sharing of the feast.
Also be like a man in how you greet
The suffering that makes your young face thin.
Be not perturbed if you are called to fight.
Only a fool thinks life was made his way,
A fool or the daughter of a wealthy house.
Husband yourself, but never stale your mind
With prudence or with doubting. I could wish
You saw my body slipping from the chair
Tomorrow. You'd remember that, my son,
And would not weigh the cost of our struggle
Against the product as a poor wife does.
But I'll not break your sleep with such a nightmare.
You looked so happy when you lay asleep . . .

But I have neither strength nor room for all
These thoughts. One single thought's enough
To fill immensity. I drop my pen. . . .

I hope this letter finds you in good health,
My son, my comrade. Will you give my love
To Inez and your mother and my friends.
Bartolo also sends his greetings to you.
I would have written better and more simple
Except my head spins like a dancing top
And my hand trembles . . . I am Oh, so weak. . . .

THE SENTRY

I have begun to die.
For now at last I know
That there is no escape
From Night. Not any dream
Nor breathless images of sleep
Touch my bat's-eyes. I hang
Leathery-arid from the hidden roof
Of Night, and sleeplessly
I watch within Sleep's province.
I have left
The lovely bodies of the boy and girl
Deep in each other's placid arms;
And I have left
The beautiful lanes of sleep
That barefoot lovers follow to this last
Cold shore of thought I guard.
I have begun to die
And the guns' implacable silence
Is my black interim, my youth and age,
In the flower of fury, the folded poppy,
Night.

Alun
Lewis

AS A PLANE TREE BY THE WATER

Robert
Lowell

Darkness has called to darkness, and disgrace
Elbows about our windows in this planned
Babel of Boston where our money talks
And multiplies the darkness of a land

[113]

Of preparation where the Virgin walks
And roses spiral her enamelled face
Or fall to splinters on unwatered streets.
Our Lady of Babylon, go by, go by,
I was once the apple of your eye;
Flies, flies are on the plane tree, on the streets.

The flies, the flies, the flies of Babylon
Buzz in my ear-drums while the devil's long
Dirge of the people detonates the hour
For floating cities where his golden tongue
Enchants the masons of the Babel Tower
To raise tomorrow's city to the sun
That never sets upon these hell-fire streets
Of Boston, where the sunlight is a sword
Striking at the withholder of the Lord:
Flies, flies are on the plane tree, on the streets.

Flies strike the miraculous waters of the iced
Atlantic and the eyes of Bernadette
Who saw Our Lady standing in the cave
At Massabielle, saw her so squarely that
Her vision put out reason's eyes. The grave
Is open-mouthed and swallowed up in Christ.
O walls of Jericho! And all the streets
To our Atlantic wall are singing: 'Sing,
Sing for the resurrection of the King.'
Flies, flies are on the plane tree, on the streets.

THE DEAD IN EUROPE

After the planes unloaded, we fell down
Buried together, unmarried men and women;
Not crown of thorns, not iron, not Lombard crown,
Not grilled and spindle spires pointing to heaven
Could save us. Raise us, Mother, we fell down
Here hugger-mugger in the jellied fire:
Our sacred earth in our day was our curse.

Our Mother, shall we rise on Mary's day
In Maryland, wherever corpses married
Under the rubble, bundled together? Pray
For us whom the blockbusters married and buried;
When Satan scatters us on Rising-day,
O Mother, snatch our bodies from the fire:
Our sacred earth in our day was our curse.

Mother, my bones are trembling and I hear
The earth's reverberations and the trumpet
Bleating into my shambles. Shall I bear,
(O Mary!) unmarried man and powder-puppet,
Witness to the Devil? Mary, hear,
O Mary, marry earth, sea, air and fire;
Our sacred earth in our day is our curse.

*Robert
Lowell*

THE LIBERTINE

*Louis
MacNeice*

In the old days with married women's stockings
Twisted round his bedpost he felt himself a gay
Dog but now his liver has begun to groan,

Now that pick-ups are the order of the day:
O leave me easy, leave me alone.

Voluptuary in his 'teens and cynic in his twenties,
He ran through women like a child through growing
    hay
Looking for a lost toy whose capture might atone
For his own guilt and the cosmic disarray:
O leave me easy, leave me alone.

He never found the toy and has forgotten the faces,
Only remembers the props . . . a scent-spray
Beside the bed or a milk-white telephone
Or through the triple ninon the acrid trickle of day:
O leave me easy, leave me alone.

Long fingers over the gunwale, hair in a hair-net,
Furs in January, cartwheel hats in May,
And after the event the wish to be alone—
Angels, goddesses, bitches, all have edged away:
O leave me easy, leave me alone.

So now, in middle age, his erotic programme
Torn in two, if after such a delay
An accident should offer him his own
Fulfilment in a woman, still he would say:
O leave me easy, leave me alone.

SUICIDE

He had fought for the wrong causes,
Had married the wrong wife,
Had invested rashly, had lost
His health and his reputation,
His fortune and his looks.

Who in his youth had gone
Walking on the crown of the road
Under delectable trees
And over irresponsible moors
To find the rainbow's end;

And was now, at forty-nine,
Living in a half-timbered
Cottage with a pale
Mistress and some gardening
Books and a life of Napoleon.

When she left him he took
The shears and clipped the hedge
And then taking his rifle
As if for duck went out
Walking on the crown of the road.

*Louis
MacNiece*

SONG

My dark-headed Käthchen, my spit-kitten darling,
You stick in my mind like an arrow of barley;
You stick in my mind like a burr on a bear,
And you drive me distracted by not being here.

*John
Manifold*

I think of you singing when dullards are talking,
I think of you fighting when fools are provoking;
To think of you now makes me faint on my feet,
And you tear me to pieces by being so sweet.

The heart in my chest like a colt in a noose
Goes plunging and straining, but it's no bloody use;
It's no bloody use, but you stick in my mind,
And you tear me to pieces by being so kind.

HIS SHIELD

Marianne
Moore

The pin-swin or spine-swine
(the edgehog miscalled hedgehog) with
        all his edges out,
    echidna and echinoderm in distressed-
pincushion thorn-fur coats,
        the spiny pig or porcupine,
            the rhino with horned snout,—
    everthing is battle-dressed.

        Pig-fur won't do, I'll wrap
myself in salamander-skin
        like Presbyter John.
    A lizard in the midst of flames, a firebrand
that is life, asbestos-
        eyed asbestos-eared with tattooed nap
            and permanent pig on
    the instep; he can withstand

[118]

fire and won't drown. In his
unconquerable country of
        unpompous gusto,
    gold was so common none considered it; greed
and flattery were
        unknown. Though rubies large as tennis-
            balls conjoined in streams so
    that the mountain seemed to bleed,

        the inextinguishable
salamander styled himself but
        presbyter. His shield
    was his humility. In Carpasian
linen coat, flanked by his
        household lion-cubs and sable
            retinue, he revealed
    a formula safer than

        an armorer's: the power of relinquishing
what one would keep; that is freedom.
        Become dinosaur-
    skulled, quilled or salamander-wooled, more iron-
        shod
and javelin-dressed than
        a hedgehog battalion of steel; but be
            dull. Don't be envied or
    armed with a measuring-rod.

VERY LIKE A WHALE

Ogden
Nash

One thing that literature would be greatly the better
for
Would be a more restricted employment by authors
of simile and metaphor.
Authors of all races, be they Greeks, Romans,
Teutons or Celts,
Can't seem just to say that anything is the thing it is
but have to go out of their way to say that it is like
something else.
What does it mean when we are told
That the Assyrian came down like a wolf on the fold?
In the first place, George Gordon Byron had had
enough experience
To know that it probably wasn't just one Assyrian, it
was a lot of Assyrians.
However, as too many arguments are apt to induce
apoplexy and thus hinder longevity,
We'll let it pass as one Assyrian for the sake of
brevity.
Now then, this particular Assyrian, the one whose
cohorts were gleaming in purple and gold.
Just what does the poet mean when he says he came
down like a wolf on the fold?
In heaven and earth more than is dreamed of in our
philosophy there are a great many things,
But I don't imagine that among them there is a wolf
with purple and gold cohorts or purple and gold
anythings.
No, no, Lord Byron, before I'll believe that this

Assyrian was actually like a wolf I must have some kind of proof;

Did he run on all fours and did he have a hairy tail and a big red mouth and big white teeth and did he say Woof woof woof?

Frankly I think it very unlikely, and all you were entitled to say, at the very most,

Was that the Assyrian cohorts came down like a lot of Assyrian cohorts about to destroy the Hebrew host.

But that wasn't fancy enough for Lord Byron, oh dear me no, he had to invent a lot of figures of speech and then interpolate them,

With the result that whenever you mention Old Testament soldiers to people they say Oh yes, they're the ones that a lot of wolves dressed up in gold and purple ate them.

That's the kind of thing that's being done all the time by poets, from Homer to Tennyson;

They're always comparing ladies to lilies and veal to venison,

And they always say things like that the snow is a white blanket after a winter storm.

Oh it is, is it, all right then, you sleep under a six-inch blanket of snow and I'll sleep under a half-inch blanket of unpoetical blanket material and we'll see which one keeps warm,

And after that maybe you'll begin to comprehend dimly

What I mean by too much metaphor and simile.

IN TIME OF PESTILENCE

*Thomas
Nashe*

Adieu! farewell earth's bliss!
This world uncertain is:
Fond are life's lustful joys,
Death proves them all but toys.
None from his darts can fly:
I am sick, I must die.
            Lord, have mercy on us!

Rich men, trust not in wealth!
Gold cannot buy you health;
Physic himself must fade;
All things to end are made;
The plague full swift goes by:
I am sick, I must die.
            Lord, have mercy on us!

Beauty is but a flower
Which wrinkles will devour:
Brightness falls from the air;
Queens have died young and fair;
Dust hath closed Helen's eye:
I am sick, I must die.
            Lord, have mercy on us!

Strength stoops unto the grave,
Worms feed on Hector brave,
Swords may not fight with fate,
Earth still holds ope her gate.

Come, come, the bells do cry,
I am sick, I must die.
>> *Lord, have mercy on us!*

Wit with his wantonness
Tasteth death's bitterness:
Hell's executioner
Hath no ears for to hear
What vain art can reply:
I am sick, I must die.
>> *Lord, have mercy on us!*

Haste, therefore, each degree
To welcome destiny:
Heaven is our heritage,
Earth but a player's stage:
Mount we unto the sky.
I am sick, I must die.
>> *Lord, have mercy on us!*

PRAYER FOR THE SPEEDY END OF THREE GREAT MISFORTUNES

Frank O'Connor

There be three things seeking my death,
All at my heels run wild—
Hang them, oh God, all three!—
Devil, maggot and child.

So much does each of them crave
    The morsel that falls to his share
He cares not a thraneen what
    Falls to the other pair.

If the devil that crafty man
    Can capture my sprightly soul,
My money may go to my children,
    My flesh to the worm in the hole.

My children think more of the money
    That falls to them when I die,
Than a soul that they could not spend,
    A body that none would buy.

And how would the maggots fare
    On a soul too thin to eat
And money too tough to chew?
    They must have my body for meat.

Christ, speared by a fool that was blind,
    Christ, nailed to a naked tree,
Since these three are waiting my end,
    Hang them, oh Christ, all three!

STRANGE MEETING

*Wilfred
Owen*

It seemed that out of the battle I escaped
Down some profound dull tunnel, long since scooped
Through granites which Titanic wars had groined.

Yet also there encumbered sleepers groaned,
Too fast in thought or death to be bestirred.
Then, as I probed them, one sprang up, and stared
With piteous recognition in fixed eyes,
Lifting distressful hands as if to bless.
And by his smile, I knew that sullen hall,
By his dead smile I knew we stood in Hell.
With a thousand pains that vision's face was grained;
Yet no blood reached there from the upper ground,
And no guns thumped, or down the flues made moan,
'Strange, friend,' I said, 'here is no cause to mourn.'
'None,' said the other, 'save the undone years,
The hopelessness. Whatever hope is yours,
Was my life also; I went hunting wild
After the wildest beauty in the world,
Which lies not calm in eyes, or braided hair,
But mocks the steady running of the hour,
And if it grieves, grieves richlier than here.
For by my glee might many men have laughed,
And of my weeping something has been left,
Which must die now. I mean the truth untold,
The pity of war, the pity war distilled.
Now men will go content with what we spoiled.
Or, discontent, boil bloody, and be spilled.
They will be swift with swiftness of the tigress,
None will break ranks, though nations trek from
    progress.
Courage was mine, and I had mystery,
Wisdom was mine, and I had mastery;
To miss the march of this retreating world
Into vain citadels that are not walled.

Then, when much blood had clogged their chariot-
    wheels
I would go up and wash them from sweet wells,
Even with truths that lie too deep for taint.
I would have poured my spirit without stint
But not through wounds; not on the cess of war.
Foreheads of men have bled where no wounds were.
I am the enemy you killed, my friend.
I knew you in this dark; for so you frowned
Yesterday through me as you jabbed and killed
I parried; but my hands were loath and cold.
Let us sleep now. . . .'

William
Plomer

A RIGHT-OF-WAY: 1865

(An old bass-viol was lately bought for a few shillings
at a farm sale not a thousand miles from Mellstock.
Pasted on the inside of it was the following poem in
a well-known handwriting. It is regretted that technical difficulties prevent its reproduction in facsimile.)

    Decades behind me
      When courting took more time,
  In Tuphampton ewe-leaze I mind me
      Two trudging aforetime:
A botanist he, in quest of a sought-after fleabane,
Wheedling his leman with 'Do you love *me*, Jane?'

Yestreen with bowed back
  (To hike now is irksome),
Hydroptic and sagging the cloud-wrack,
  I spied in the murk some
Wayfarer myopic Linnaeus-wise quizzing the
  quitches
And snooping at simples and worts in the ditches.

  Remarked he, 'A path here
  I seek to discover,
A right-of-way bang through this garth here,
  Where elsewhiles a lover
I prinked with a pocket herbarium, necked I and
  cuddled:
Now I'm all mud-besprent, bored and be-puddled.

  'I'm long past my noon-time.
  The Unweeting Planner
Again proffers bale for one's boon-time
  By tossing a spanner
Or crowbar into the works without recking the cost,
  sir.
At eighty,' intoned he, 'life is a frost, sir.

  'When erst here I tarried
  I knew not my steady
Had coolly, concurrently married
  Three husbands already,
Nor learnt I till later, what's more, that all three were
  brothers,
Though sprang they, it seems, of disparate mothers.

'Well, we two inspected
    The flora of Wessex;
  More specimens had we collected
    Had she pondered less sex;
We botanized little that year. . . . But I must be
    wending;
My analyst hints at amnesia impending.'

*William
Plomer*

THE FLYING BUM: 1944

In the vegetarian guest-house
All was frolic, feast and fun,
Eager voices were enquiring
'Are the nettle cutlets done?'
Peals of vegetarian laughter,
Husky wholesome wholemeal bread,
Will the evening finish with a
Rush of cocoa to the head?

Yes, you've guessed; it's Minnie's birthday,
Hence the frolic, hence the feast.
Are there calories in custard?
There are vitamins in yeast.
Kate is here and Tom her hubby,
Ex-commissioner for oaths,
She is mad on Christian Science,
Parsnip flan he simply loathes.

[128]

And Mr Croaker, call him Arthur,
Such a keen philatelist,
Making sheep's-eyes at Louisa
(After dinner there'll be whist)—
Come, sit down, the soup is coming,
All of docks and darnels made,
Drinks a health to dear old Minnie
In synthetic lemonade.

Dentures champing juicy lettuce,
Champing macerated bran,
Oh the imitation rissoles!
Oh the food untouched by man!
Look, an imitation sausage
Made of monkey-nuts and spice,
Prunes tonight and semolina,
Wrinkled prunes, unpolished rice.

Yards of guts absorbing jellies,
Bellies filling up with nuts,
Carbohydrates jostling proteins
Out of intestinal ruts;
Peristalsis calls for roughage,
Haulms and fibres, husks and grit,
Nature's way to open bowels,
Maybe—let them practise it.

'Hark, I hear an air-raid warning!'
'Take no notice, let 'em come.'
'Who'll say grace?' 'Another walnut?'
'Listen, what's that distant hum?'

'Bomb or no bomb,' stated Minnie,
'Lips unsoiled by beef or beer
We shall use to greet our Maker
When he sounds the Great All-Clear.'

When the flying bomb exploded
Minnie's wig flew off her pate,
Half a curtain, like a tippet,
Wrapped itself round bony Kate,
Plaster landed on Louisa,
Tom fell headlong on the floor,
And a spurt of lukewarm custard
Lathered Mr Croaker's jaw.

All were spared by glass and splinters
But, the loud explosion past,
Greater was the shock impending
Even than the shock of blast—
Blast we veterans know as freakish
Gave this feast its final course,
Planted bang upon the table
A lightly roasted rump of horse.

Ezra Pound

SOIRÉE

Upon learning that the mother wrote verses,
And that the father wrote verses,
And that the youngest son was in a publisher's office,

[130]

And that the friend of the second daughter was under-
    going a novel,
The young American pilgrim
Exclaimed:
        'This is a darn'd clever bunch!'

CLARA

*Ezra
Pound*

At sixteen she was a potential celebrity
With a distaste for caresses.
She now writes to me from a convent;
Her life is obscure and troubled;
Her second husband will not divorce her;
Her mind is, as ever, uncultivated,
And no issue presents itself.
She does not desire her children,
Or any more children.
Her ambition is vague and indefinite,
She will neither stay in, nor come out.

THE RIVER-MERCHANT'S WIFE:
A LETTER

*Ezra
Pound*

While my hair was still cut straight across my fore-
    head
I played about the front gate, pulling flowers.
You came by on bamboo stilts, playing horse,
You walked about my seat, playing with blue plums.
And we went on living in the village of Chokan:
Two small people, without dislike or suspicion.

At fourteen I married My Lord you.
I never laughed, being bashful.
Lowering my head, I looked at the wall.
Called to, a thousand times, I never looked back.

At fifteen I stopped scowling,
I desired my dust to be mingled with yours
Forever and forever and forever.
Why should I climb the look out?

At sixteen you departed,
You went into far Ku-to-yen, by the river of swirling
 eddies,
And you have been gone five months.
The monkeys make sorrowful noise overhead.

You dragged your feet when you went out.
By the gate now, the moss is grown, the different
 mosses,
Too deep to clear them away!
The leaves fall early this autumn, in wind.
The paired butterflies are already yellow with August
Over the grass in the West garden;

They hurt me. I grow older.
If you are coming down through the narrows of the
 river Kiang,
Please let me know beforehand,
And I will come out to meet you
                As far as Cho-fu-Sa.

HIS PILGRIMAGE
Supposed to be Written by One at the Point of Death

Give me my Scallop shell of quiet,
My staff of Faith to walk upon,
My Scrip of Joy, Immortal diet,
My bottle of salvation:
My Gown of Glory, hope's true gage,
And thus I'll take my pilgrimage.

Blood must be my body's balmer,
No other balm will there be given
Whilst my soul like a white Palmer
Travels to the land of heaven,
Over the silver mountains,
Where spring the Nectar fountains:

And there I'll kiss
The Bowl of bliss,
And drink my eternal fill
On every milken hill.
My soul will be a-dry before,
But after it, will ne'er thirst more.

And by the happy blissful way
More peaceful Pilgrims I shall see,
That have shook off their gowns of clay,
And go apparell'd fresh like me.
I'll bring them first
To slake their thirst,

*Sir Walter
Raleigh*

And then to taste those Nectar suckets
At the clear wells
Where sweetness dwells,
Drawn up by Saints in Chrystal buckets.

And when our bottles and all we
Are fill'd with immortality:
Then the holy paths we'll travel
Strew'd with Rubies thick as gravel,
Ceilings of Diamonds, Sapphire floors,
High walls of Coral and Pearl Bow'rs.

From thence to heaven's Bribeless hall
Where no corrupted voices brawl,
No Conscience molten into gold,
Nor forg'd accusers bought and sold,
No cause deferr'd, nor vain spent Journey,
For there Christ is the Kings Attorney:
Who pleads for all without degrees,
And he hath Angels, but no fees.

When the grand twelve million Jury,
Of our sins with sinful fury,
'Gainst our souls black verdicts give,
Christ pleads his death, and then we live,
Be thou my speaker, taintless pleader,
Unblotted Lawyer, true proceeder,
Thou movest salvation even for alms:
Not with a bribed Lawyer's palms.

And this is my eternal plea,
To him that made Heaven, Earth and Sea,
Seeing my flesh must die so soon,
And want a head to dine next noon,
Just at the stroke when my veins start and spread
Set on my soul an everlasting head.
Then am I ready like a palmer fit,
To tread those blest paths which before I writ.

BELLS FOR JOHN WHITESIDE'S DAUGHTER

*John
Crowe
Ransom*

There was such speed in her little body,
And such lightness in her footfall,
It is no wonder her brown study
Astonishes us all.

Her wars were bruited in our high window.
We looked among orchard trees and beyond,
Where she took arms against her shadow,
Or harried unto the pond

The lazy geese, like a snow cloud
Dripping their snow on the green grass,
Tricking and stopping, sleepy and proud,
Who cried in goose, Alas,

For the tireless heart within the little
Lady with rod that made them rise
From their noon apple-dreams and scuttle
Goose-fashion under the skies!

But now go the bells, and we are ready,
In one house we are sternly stopped
To say we are vexed at her brown study,
Lying so primly propped.

*John
Crowe
Ransom*

JUDITH OF BETHULIA

Beautiful as the flying legend of some leopard
She had not yet chosen her great captain or prince
Depositary to her flesh, and our defence;
And a wandering beauty is a blade out of its scabbard.
You know how dangerous, gentlemen of threescore?
May you know it yet ten more.

Nor by process of veiling she grew the less fabulous.
Grey or blue veils, we were desperate to study
The invincible emanations of her white body,
And the winds at her ordered raiment were ominous.
Might she walk in the market, sit in the council of
   soldiers?
Only of the extreme elders.

But a rare chance was the girl's then, when the
   Invader
Trumpeted from the south, and rumbled from the
   north,
Beleaguered the city from four quarters of the earth
Our soldiery too craven and sick to aid her—
Where were the arms could countervail this horde?
Her beauty was the sword.

She sat with the elders, and proved on their blear
     visage
How bright was the weapon unrusted in her keeping,
While he lay surfeiting on their harvest heaping,
Wasting the husbandry of their rarest vintage—
And dreaming of the broad-breasted dames for
     concubine?
These floated on his wine.

He was lapped with bay-leaves, and grass and fumiter
     weed,
And from under the wine-film encountered his mortal
     vision,
For even within his tent she accomplished his derision;
She loosed one veil and another, standing unafraid;
And he perished. Nor brushed her with even so much
     as a daisy?
She found his destruction easy.

The heathen are all perished. The victory was
     furnished,
We smote them hiding in our vineyards, barns,
     annexes,
And now their white bones clutter the holes of foxes,
And the chieftain's head, with grinning sockets, and
     varnished—
Is it hung on the sky with a hideous epitaphy?
No, the woman keeps the trophy.

May God send unto our virtuous lady her prince.
It is stated she went reluctant to that orgy,

Yet a madness fevers our young men, and not the
    clergy
Nor the elders have turned them unto modesty since.
Inflamed by the thought of her naked beauty with
    desire?
Yes, and chilled with fear and despair.

PARTING, WITHOUT A SEQUEL

*John
Crowe
Ransom*

She has finished and sealed the letter
At last, which he so richly has deserved,
Without characters venomous and hatefully curved,
And nothing could be better.

But even as she gave it
Saying to the blue-capped functioner of doom,
'Into his hands,' she hoped the leering groom
Might somewhere lose and leave it.

Then all the blood
Forsook the face. She was too pale for tears,
Observing the ruin of her younger years.
She went and stood

Under her father's vaunting oak
Who kept his peace in wind and sun, and glistened
Stoical in the rain; to whom she listened
If he spoke.

[138]

And now the agitation of the rain
Rasped his sere leaves, and he talked low and gentle
Reproaching the wan daughter by the lintel;
Ceasing and beginning again.

Away went the messenger's bicycle,
His serpent's track went up the hill forever,
And all the time she stood there hot as fever
And cold as any icicle.

CHARD WHITLOW
Mr Eliot's Sunday Evening Postscript

*Henry
Reed*

As we get older we do not get any younger.
Seasons return, and today I am fifty-five,
And this time last year I was fifty-four,
And this time next year I shall be sixty-two.
And I cannot say I should care (to speak for myself)
To see my time over again—if you can call it time,
Fidgeting uneasily under a draughty stair,
Or counting sleepless nights in the crowded Tube.

There are certain precautions—though none of them
    very reliable—
Against the blast from bombs, or the flying splinter,
But not against the blast from Heaven, *vento dei venti*,
The wind within a wind, unable to speak for wind;
And the frigid burnings of purgatory will not be
    touched
By any emollient.

I think you will find this put,
Far better than I could ever hope to express it,
In the words of Kharma: 'It is, we believe,
Idle to hope that the simple stirrup-pump
Can extinguish hell.'

Oh, listeners,
And you especially who have switched off the
    wireless,
And sit in Stoke or Basingstoke, listening apprecia-
    tively to the silence
(Which is also the silence of hell), pray not for
    yourselves but your souls.

And pray for me also under the draughty stair.
As we get older we do not get any younger.

And pray for Kharma under the holy mountain.

Henry Reed

NAMING OF PARTS
from *Lessons of the War*

Today we have naming of parts. Yesterday,
We had daily cleaning. And tomorrow morning,
We shall have what to do after firing. But today,
Today we have naming of parts. Japonica
Glistens like coral in all of the neighbouring gardens,
    And today we have naming of parts.

This is the lower sling swivel. And this
Is the upper sling swivel, whose use you will see,
When you are given your slings. And this is the
    piling swivel,
Which in your case you have not got. The branches
Hold in the gardens their silent, eloquent gestures,
    Which in our case we have not got.

This is the safety-catch, which is always released
With an easy flick of the thumb. And please do not
    let me
See anyone using his finger. You can do it quite easy
If you have any strength in your thumb. The
    blossoms
Are fragile and motionless, never letting anyone see
    Any of them using their finger.

And this you can see is the bolt. The purpose of this
Is to open the breech, as you see. We can slide it
Rapidly backwards and forwards: we call this
Easing the spring. And rapidly backwards and for-
    wards
The early bees are assaulting and fumbling the flowers:
    They call it easing the Spring.

They call it easing the Spring: it is perfectly easy
If you have any strength in your thumb: like the bolt,
And the breech, and the cocking-piece, and the point
    of balance,

Which in our case we have not got; and the almond-
blossom
Silent in all of the gardens and the bees going backwards and forwards,
For today we have naming of parts.

*James
Reeves*

THE LITTLE BROTHER

God! how they plague his life, the three damned
sisters,
Throwing stones at him out of the cherry trees,
Pulling his hair, smudging his exercises,
Whispering. How passionately he sees
His spilt minnows flounder in the grass.

There will be sisters subtler far than these,
Baleful and dark, with slender, cared-for hands,
Who will not smirk and babble in the trees,
But feed him with sweet words and provocations,
And in his sleep practise their sorceries,
Appearing in the form of ragged clouds
And at the corners of malignant seas.

As with his wounded life he goes alone
To the world's end, where even tears freeze,
He will in bitter memory and remorse
Hear the lost sisters innocently tease.

RICHARD CORY

Whenever Richard Cory went down town,
We people on the pavement looked at him:
He was a gentleman from sole to crown,
Clean favored, and imperially slim.

And he was always quietly arrayed,
And he was always human when he talked;
But still he fluttered pulses when he said,
'Good morning,' and he glittered when he walked.

And he was rich—yes, richer than a king—
And admirably schooled in every grace:
In fine, we thought that he was everything
To make us wish that we were in his place.

So on we worked, and waited for the light,
And went without the meat, and cursed the bread;
And Richard Cory, one calm summer night,
Went home and put a bullet through his head.

*Edwin
Arlington
Robinson*

LENT

*W. R.
Rodgers*

Mary Magdalene, that easy woman,
Saw, from the shore, the seas
Beat against the hard stone of Lent,
Crying: 'Weep, seas, weep
For yourselves that cannot dent me more.

[143]

O more than all these, more crabbed than all stones,
And cold, make me, who once
Could leap like water, Lord. Take me
As one who owes
Nothing to what she was. Ah, naked.

My waves of scent, my petticoats of foam
Put from me and rebut;
Disown. And that salt lust stave off
That slavered me—O
Let it whiten in grief against the stones

And outer reefs of me. Utterly doff,
Nor leave the lightest veil
Of feeling to heave or soften.
Nothing cares this heart
What hardness crates it now or coffins.

Over the balconies of these curved breasts
I'll no more peep to see
The light procession of my loves
Surf-riding in to me
Who now have eyes and alcoves, Lord, for Thee.'

'Room, Mary,' said He, 'ah make room for me
Who am come so cold now
To my tomb.' So, on Good Friday,
Under a frosty moon
They carried Him and laid Him in her womb.

A grave and icy mask her heart wore twice,
But on the third day it thawed,
And only a stone's-flow away
Mary saw her God.
Did you hear me? Mary saw her God!

Dance, Mary Magdalene, dance, dance and sing,
For unto you is born
This day a King. 'Lady', said He,
'To you who relent
I bring back the petticoat and the bottle of scent.'

CAROL

W. R.
Rodgers

Deep in the fading leaves of night
There lay the flower that darkness knows,
Till winter stripped and brought to light
The most incomparable Rose
That blows, that blows.

The flashing mirrors of the snow
Keep turning and returning still:
To see the lovely child below
And hold him is their only will;
Keep still, keep still.

And to let go his very cry
The clinging echoes are so slow
That still his wail they multiply
Though he lie singing now below
So low, so low.

Even the doves forget to grieve
And gravely to his greeting fly
And the lone places that they leave
All follow and are standing by
On high, on high.

John
Short
CAROL

There was a Boy bedded in bracken,
    Like to a sleeping snake all curled he lay;
      On his thin navel turned this spinning sphere,
        Each feeble finger fetched seven suns away.
        He was not dropped in good-for-lambing
          weather,
        He took no suck when shook buds sing
          together,
        But he is come in cold-as-workhouse weather,
          Poor as a Salford child.

STILL FALLS THE RAIN
Edith
Sitwell
       The Raids, 1940.   *Night and Dawn.*

Still falls the Rain—
Dark as the world of man, black as our loss—
Blind as the nineteen hundred and forty nails
Upon the Cross.

Still falls the Rain
With a sound like the pulse of the heart that is
    changed to the hammer-beat
In the Potter's Field, and the sound of the impious
    feet

On the Tomb:
                    Still falls the Rain
In the Field of Blood where the small hopes breed
    and the human brain
Nurtures its greed, that worm with the brow of Cain.

Still falls the Rain
At the feet of the Starved Man hung upon the Cross.
Christ that each day, each night, nails there, have
    mercy on us—
On Dives and on Lazarus:
Under the Rain the sore and the gold are as one.

Still falls the Rain—
Still falls the Blood from the Starved Man's wounded
    Side:
He bears in His Heart all wounds,—those of the light
    that died,
The last faint spark
In the self-murdered heart, the wounds of the sad
    uncomprehending dark,
The wounds of the baited bear,—
The blind and weeping bear whom the keepers beat
On his helpless flesh . . . the tears of the hunted hare.

[147]

Still falls the Rain—
Then—O Ile leape up to my God: who pulles me
    doune—
See, see where Christ's blood streames in the firma-
    ment:
It flows from the Brow we nailed upon the tree
Deep to the dying, to the thirsting heart
That holds the fires of the world,—dark-smirched
    with pain
As Caesar's laurel crown.

Then sounds the voice of One who like the heart of
    man
Was once a child who among beasts has lain—
'Still do I love, still shed my innocent light, my
    Blood, for thee.'

A GLASS OF BEER

*James
Stephens*

The lanky hank of a she in the inn over there
Nearly killed me for asking the loan of a glass of beer:
May the devil grip the whey-faced slut by the hair,
And beat bad manners out of her skin for a year.

That parboiled imp, with the hardest jaw you will see
On virtue's path, and a voice that would rasp the
    dead,
Came roaring and raging the minute she looked at me,
And threw me out of the house on the back of my
    head!

If I asked her master he'd give me a cask a day;
But she, with the beer at hand, not a gill would
  arrange!
May she marry a ghost and bear him a kitten, and
  may
The High King of Glory permit her to get the mange.

MIDNIGHT

*James
Stephens*

And then I wakened up in such a fright;
  I thought I heard a movement in the room
But did not dare to look; I snuggled right
  Down underneath the bedclothes—then the boom
Of a tremendous voice said, '*Sit up, lad,
  And let me see your face.*' So up I sat,
Although I didn't want to. I was glad
  I did though, for it was an angel that
Had called me, and he said, he'd come to know
  Was I the boy who wouldn't say his prayers
Nor do his sums, and that I'd have to go
  Straight down to hell because of such affairs.
. . . I said I'd be converted and do good
If he would let me off—he said he would.

THE BREWER'S MAN

*L. A. G.
Strong*

Have I a wife? Bedam I have!
  But we was badly mated.
I hit her a great clout one night,
  And now we're separated.

[149]

And mornin's, going to me work
   I meets her on the quay:
'Good mornin' to ye, ma'am!' says I:
   'To hell with ye!' says she.

THE UNKNOWN BIRD

Edward Thomas

Three lovely notes he whistled, too soft to be heard
If others sang; but others never sang
In the great beech-wood all that May and June.
No one saw him: I alone could hear him
Though many listened. Was it but four years
Ago? or five? He never came again.

Oftenest when I heard him I was alone,
Nor could I ever make another hear.
La-la-la! he called, seeming far-off—
As if a cock crowed past the edge of the world,
As if the bird or I were in a dream.
Yet that he travelled through the trees and sometimes
Neared me, was plain, though somehow distant still
He sounded. All the proof is—I told men
What I had heard.

         I never knew a voice,
Man, beast, or bird, better than this. I told
The naturalists; but neither had they heard
Anything like the notes that did so haunt me,
I had them clear by heart and have them still.
Four years, or five, have made no difference. Then

[150]

As now that La-la-la! was bodiless sweet:
Sad more than joyful it was, if I must say
That it was one or other, but if sad
'Twas sad only with joy too, too far off
For me to taste it. But I cannot tell
If truly never anything but fair
The days were when he sang, as now they seem.
This surely I know, that I who listened then,
Happy sometimes, sometimes suffering
A heavy body and a heavy heart,
Now straightway, if I think of it, become
Light as that bird wandering beyond my shore.

THE OWL

Edward Thomas

Downhill I came, hungry, and yet not starved;
Cold, yet had heat within me that was proof
Against the North wind; tired, yet so that rest
Had seemed the sweetest thing under a roof.

Then at the inn I had food, fire, and rest,
Knowing how hungry, cold, and tired was I.
All of the night was quite barred out except
An owl's cry, a most melancholy cry

Shaken out long and clear upon the hill,
No merry note, nor cause of merriment,
But one telling me plain what I escaped
And others could not, that night, as in I went.

[151]

And salted was my food, and my repose,
Salted and sobered, too, by the bird's voice
Speaking for all who lay under the stars,
Soldiers and poor, unable to rejoice.

A LOVER'S WORDS

*Vernon
Watkins*

Come down, dear love, be quick.
Now must our limbs' great follies
Fly through the zodiac
Where colts race with fillies.
Night, and the light-shafts fly.
Noon, and the stars are thick.
Naked through Earth and Sky
Come down, and hurl time back.

Tell the sun to rise.
Tell all the birds to sing.
Then cover the brightening skies
With a tented covering,
That under the sheet awake
The naked limbs flying
Bend, till the axle break,
All but their true lying.

Dive, sun, through my hand,
And pull the waters after;
Spin the whirling land
In a silkworm's darkness, softer

Than light, a luminous net,
That we, with meteors' arms
Far under the coverlet
May wind the winds and storms.

Beautiful head, lie still.
Light beats the pillows.
The cock crows, shrill:
That cry no lover follows.
Shining with glow-worms' light
We shape the world to our will,
Twined, hidden from sight
With blind-moles under the hill.

THE COLLIER

*Vernon
Watkins*

When I was born on Amman hill
A dark bird crossed the sun.
Sharp on the floor the shadow fell;
I was the youngest son.

And when I went to the County School
I worked in a shaft of light.
In the wood of the desk I cut my name:
Dai for Dynamite.

The tall black hills my brothers stood;
Their lessons all were done.
From the door of the school when I ran out
They frowned to watch me run.

The slow grey bells they rung a chime
Surly with grief or age.
Clever or clumsy, lad or lout,
All would look for a wage.

I learnt the valley flowers' names
And the rough bark knew my knees.
I brought home trout from the river
And spotted eggs from the trees.

A coloured coat I was given to wear
Where the lights of the rough land shone.
Still jealous of my favour
The tall black hills looked on.

They dipped my coat in the blood of a kid
And they cast me down a pit,
And although I crossed with strangers
There was no way up from it.

Soon as I went from the County School
I worked in a shaft. Said Jim,
'You will get your chain of gold, my lad,
But not for a likely time.'

And one said, 'Jack was not raised up
When the wind blew out the light
Though he interpreted their dreams
And guessed their fears by night.'

[154]

And Tom, he shivered his leper's lamp
For the stain that round him grew;
And I heard mouths pray in the after-damp
When the picks would not break through.

They changed words there in darkness
And still through my head they run,
And white on my limbs is the linen sheet
And gold on my neck the sun.

THE BURIED CHILD
Epilogue to 'Deserted House'

*Dorothy
Wellesley*

He is not dead nor liveth
The little child in the grave,
And men have known for ever
That he walketh again;
They hear him November evenings,
When acorns fall with the rain.

Deep in the hearts of men
Within his tomb he lieth,
And when the heart is desolate
He desolate sigheth.

Teach me then the heart of the dead child,
Who, holding a tulip, goeth
Up the stairs in his little grave-shift,
Sitting down in his little chair
By his biscuit and orange,
In the nursery he knoweth.

Teach me all that the child who knew life
And the quiet of death,
To the croon of the cradle-song
By his brother's crib
In the deeps of the nursery dusk
To his mother saith.

W. B.
Yeats

THREE THINGS

'O cruel Death, give three things back,'
Sang a bone upon the shore;
'A child found all a child can lack,
Whether of pleasure or of rest,
Upon the abundance of my breast':
A bone wave-whitened and dried in the wind.

'Three dear things that women know,'
Sang a bone upon the shore;
'A man if I but held him so
When my body was alive
Found all the pleasure that life gave':
A bone wave-whitened and dried in the wind.

'The third thing that I think of yet,'
Sang a bone upon the shore,
'Is that morning when I met
Face to face my rightful man
And did after stretch and yawn':
A bone wave-whitened and dried in the wind.

HE THINKS OF HIS PAST GREATNESS WHEN A PART OF THE CONSTELLATIONS OF HEAVEN

W. B. Yeats

I have drunk ale from the Country of the Young
And weep because I know all things now:
I have been a hazel-tree, and they hung
The Pilot Star and the Crooked Plough
Among my leaves in times out of mind:
I became a rush that horses tread:
I became a man, a hater of the wind,
Knowing one, out of all things, alone, that his head
May not lie on the breast nor his lips on the hair
Of the woman that he loves, until he dies.
O beast of the wilderness, bird of the air,
Must I endure your amorous cries?

FROM 'OEDIPUS AT COLONUS'

W. B. Yeats

Endure what life God gives and ask no longer span;
Cease to remember the delights of youth, travel-
    wearied aged man;
Delight becomes death-longing if all longing else be
    vain.

Even from that delight memory treasures so,
Death, despair, division of families, all entanglements
    of mankind grow,
As that old wandering beggar and these God-hated
    children know.

In the long echoing street the laughing dancers throng,
The bride is carried to the bridegroom's chamber
  through torchlight and tumultuous song;
I celebrate the silent kiss that ends short life or long.

Never to have lived is best, ancient writers say;
Never to have drawn the breath of life, never to have
  looked into the eye of day;
The second best's a gay goodnight and quickly turn
  away.

W. B.
Yeats

FOR ANNE GREGORY

'Never shall a young man,
Thrown into despair
By those great honey-coloured
Ramparts at your ear,
Love you for yourself alone
And not your yellow hair.'

'But I can get a hair-dye
And set such colour there,
Brown, or black, or carrot,
That young men in despair
May love me for myself alone
And not my yellow hair.'

'I heard an old religious man
But yesternight declare

That he had found a text to prove
That only God, my dear,
Could love you for yourself alone
And not your yellow hair.'

LAPIS LAZULI
For Harry Clifton

W. B.
Yeats

I have heard that hysterical women say
They are sick of the palette and fiddle-bow,
Of poets that are always gay,
For everybody knows or else should know
That if nothing drastic is done
Aeroplane and Zeppelin will come out,
Pitch like King Billy bomb-balls in
Until the town lie beaten flat.

All perform their tragic play,
There struts Hamlet, there is Lear,
That's Ophelia, that Cordelia;
Yet they, should the last scene be there,
The great stage curtain about to drop,
If worthy their prominent part in the play,
Do not break up their lines to weep.
They know that Hamlet and Lear are gay;
Gaiety transfiguring all that dread.
All men have aimed at, found and lost;
Black out; Heaven blazing into the head:
Tragedy wrought to its uttermost.
Though Hamlet rambles and Lear rages,

And all the drop-scenes drop at once
Upon a hundred thousand stages,
It cannot grow by an inch or an ounce.

On their own feet they came, or on shipboard,
Camel-back, horse-back, ass-back, mule-back,
Old civilizations put to the sword.
Then they and their wisdom went to rack:
No handiwork of Callimachus,
Who handled marble as if it were bronze,
Made draperies that seemed to rise
When sea-wind swept the corner, stands;
His long lamp-chimney shaped like the stem
Of a slender palm, stood but a day;
All things fall and are built again,
And those that build them again are gay.

Two Chinamen, behind them a third,
Are carved in lapis lazuli,
Over them flies a long-legged bird,
A symbol of longevity;
The third, doubtless a serving-man,
Carries a musical instrument.

Every discoloration of the stone,
Every accidental crack or dent,
Seems a water-course or an avalanche,
Or lofty slope where it still snows
Though doubtless plum or cherry-branch
Sweetens the little half-way house
Those Chinamen climb towards, and I

Delight to imagine them seated there;
There, on the mountain and the sky,
On all the tragic scene they stare.
One asks for mournful melodies;
Accomplished fingers begin to play.
Their eyes mid many wrinkles, their eyes,
Their ancient, glittering eyes, are gay.

JOHN KINSELLA'S LAMENT FOR MRS MARY MOORE

W. B. Yeats

A bloody and a sudden end,
    Gunshot or a noose,
For Death who takes what man would keep,
    Leaves what man would lose.
He might have had my sister,
    My cousins by the score,
But nothing satisfied the fool
    But my dear Mary Moore,
None other knows what pleasures man
    At table or in bed.
What shall I do for pretty girls
    Now my old bawd is dead?

Though stiff to strike a bargain,
    Like an old Jew man,
Her bargain struck we laughed and talked
    And emptied many a can;
And O! but she had stories,
    Though not for the priest's ear,

To keep the soul of man alive,
    Banish age and care,
And being old she put a skin
    On everything she said.
What shall I do for pretty girls
    Now my old bawd is dead?

The priests have got a book that says
    But for Adam's sin
Eden's Garden would be there
    And I there within.
No expectation fails there,
    No pleasing habit ends,
No man grows old, no girl grows cold,
    But friends walk by friends.
Who quarrels over halfpennies
    That plucks the trees for bread?
What shall I do for pretty girls
    Now my old bawd is dead?

W. B.
Yeats A DIALOGUE OF SELF AND SOUL

I

My Soul. I summon to the winding ancient stair;
    Set all your mind upon the steep ascent,
    Upon the broken, crumbling battlement,
    Upon the breathless starlit air,
    Upon the star that marks the hidden pole;
    Fix every wandering thought upon
    That quarter where all thought is done:
    Who can distinguish darkness from the soul?

My Self. The consecrated blade upon my knees
Is Sato's ancient blade, still as it was,
Still razor-keen, still like a looking-glass
Unspotted by the centuries;
That flowering, silken, old embroidery, torn
From some court-lady's dress and round
The wooden scabbard bound and wound,
Can, tattered, still protect, faded adorn.

My Soul. Why should the imagination of a man
Long past his prime remember things that are
Emblematical of love and war?
Think of ancestral night that can,
If but imagination scorn the earth
And intellect its wandering
To this and that and t'other thing,
Deliver from the crime of death and birth.

My Self. Montashigi, third of this family, fashioned it
Five hundred years ago, about it lie
Flowers from I know not what embroidery—
Heart's purple—and all these I set
For emblems of the day against the tower
Emblematical of the night,
And claim as by a soldier's right
A charter to commit the crime once more.

My Soul. Such fullness in that quarter overflows
And falls into the basin of the mind
That man is stricken deaf and dumb and blind,
For intellect no longer knows
Is from the *Ought*, or *Knower* from the *Known*—

[163]

That is to say, ascends to Heaven;
Only the dead can be forgiven;
But when I think of that my tongue's a stone.

II

My Self. A living man is blind and drinks his drop.
What matter if the ditches are impure?
What matter if I live it all once more?
Endure that toil of growing up;
The ignominy of boyhood; the distress
Of boyhood changing into man;
The unfinished man and his pain
Brought face to face with his own clumsiness;

The finished man among his enemies?—
How in the name of Heaven can he escape
That defiling and disfigured shape
The mirror of malicious eyes
Casts upon his eyes until at last
He thinks that shape must be his shape?
And what's the good of an escape
If honour find him in the wintry blast?

I am content to live it all again
And yet again, if it be life to pitch
Into the frog-spawn of a blind man's ditch,
A blind man battering blind men;
Or into that most fecund ditch of all,
The folly that man does
Or must suffer, if he woos
A proud woman not kindred of his soul.

I am content to follow to its source
Every event in action or in thought;
Measure the lot; forgive myself the lot!
When such as I cast out remorse
So great a sweetness flows into the breast
We must laugh and we must sing,
We are blest by everything,
Everything we look upon is blest.

THE THREE BUSHES

*An incident from the 'Historia mei Temporis' of the
Abbé Michel de Bourdeille*

*W. B.
Yeats*

SAID lady once to lover,
'None can rely upon
A love that lacks its proper food;
And if your love were gone
How could you sing those songs of love?
I should be blamed, young man.
                    O my dear, O my dear.

'Have no lit candles in your room,'
That lovely lady said,
'That I at midnight by the clock
May creep into your bed,
For if I saw myself creep in
I think I should drop dead.'
                    O my dear, O my dear.

'I love a man in secret,
Dear chambermaid,' said she.
'I know that I must drop down dead
If he stop loving me,
Yet what could I but drop down dead
If I lost my chastity?
           O my dear, O my dear.

'So you must lie beside him
And let him think me there.
And maybe we are all the same
Where no candles are,
And maybe we are all the same
That strip the body bare.'
           O my dear, O my dear.

But no dogs barked, and midnights chimed,
And through the chime she'd say,
'That was a lucky thought of mine,
My lover looked so gay';
But heaved a sigh if the chambermaid
Looked half asleep all day.
           O my dear, O my dear.

'No, not another song,' said he,
'Because my lady came
A year ago for the first time
At midnight to my room,
And I must lie between the sheets
When the clock begins to chime.'
           O my dear, O my dear.

'A laughing, crying, sacred song,
A leching song,' they said.
Did ever men hear such a song?
No, but that day they did.
Did ever man ride such a race?
No, not until he rode.
                O my dear, O my dear.

But when his horse had put its hoof
Into a rabbit-hole
He dropped upon his head and died.
His lady saw it all
And dropped and died thereon, for she
Loved him with her soul.
                O my dear, O my dear.

The chambermaid lived long, and took
Their graves into her charge,
And there two bushes planted
That when they had grown large
Seemed sprung from but a single root
So did their roses merge.
                O my dear, O my dear.

When she was old and dying,
The priest came where she was;
She made a full confession.
Long looked he in her face,
And O he was a good man
And understood her case.
                O my dear, O my dear.

He bade them take and bury her
Beside her lady's man,
And set a rose-tree on her grave,
And now none living can,
When they have plucked a rose there,
Know where its roots began.
                    O my dear, O my dear.

Andrew
Young

PASSING THE GRAVEYARD

I see you did not try to save
The bouquet of white flowers I gave;
So fast they wither on your grave.

Why does it hurt the heart to think
Of that most bitter abrupt brink
Where the low-shouldered coffins sink?

These living bodies that we wear
So change by every seventh year
That in a new dress we appear;

Limbs, spongy brain and slogging heart,
No part remains the selfsame part;
Like streams they stay and still depart.

You slipped slow bodies in the past;
Then why should we be so aghast
You flung off the whole flesh at last?

[168]

Let him who loves you think instead
That like a woman who has wed
You undressed first and went to bed.

A PROSPECT OF DEATH

*Andrew
Young*

If it should come to this
You cannot wake me with a kiss,
Think I but sleep too late
Or once again keep a cold angry state.

So now you have been told;—
I or my breakfeast may grow cold,
But you must only say
'Why does he miss the best part of the day?'

Even then you may be wrong;
Through woods torn by a blackbird's song
My thoughts may often roam
While graver business makes me stay at home.

There will be time enough
To go back to the earth I love
Some other day that week,
Perhaps to find what all my life I seek.

So do not dream of danger;
Forgive my lateness or my anger;
You have so much forgiven,
Forgive me this or that, or Hell or Heaven.

THE SHEPHERD'S HUT

Andrew Young

The smear of blue peat smoke
That staggered on the wind and broke,
The only sign of life,
Where was the shepherd's wife,
Who left those flapping clothes to dry,
Taking no thought for her family?
For, as they bellied out
And limbs took shape and waved about,
I thought, She little knows
That ghosts are trying on her children's clothes.

INDEX OF FIRST LINES

[173]

[174]